W9-AQO-178

Twayne's English Authors Series

By Donald B. Clark

UNIVERSITY OF MISSOURI

Alexander Pope

 41

Alexander Pope

By DONALD B. CLARK

University of Missouri

Twayne Publishers, Inc. :: New York

CARNEGIE LIBRARY
LIVINGSTONE COLLEGE
SALISBURY, N. C. 28144

Copyright © 1967, by Twayne Publishers, Inc.

All Rights Reserved

Library of Congress Catalog Card Number: 66–21747

MANUFACTURED IN THE UNITED STATES OF AMERICA

821.53
Po81Yc

For M., C., and C.

73115

Preface

In the last thirty years more books and studies on Alexander Pope have appeared in print than had been published in the entire preceding century. To add one more book to this large group may seem unnecessary. Most of these studies, however, center their attention on one particular poem, or they examine a group of poems from a special point of view. In contrast, this study attempts to present a coherent, unified interpretation of Pope's major poems. It argues that the poet's vision of harmony through variety—the friendly strife—is a guiding philosophy which runs from the first work to the final version of the "Dunciad." This idea undergirds such disparate genres as the early pastoral poems and the late satires, in which man is upbraided for breaking that harmony which is nature. In tracing this principle through the poetry of Alexander Pope, I have attempted also to note his development as a poet, largely in terms of his increasing mastery of the use of allusion and metaphor.

I have consciously minimized historical, biographical, and philosophical backgrounds as ends in themselves. When a knowledge of these is necessary to the interpretation of a poem by a modern reader, the relevant material is presented; otherwise, references in the Notes and Bibliography direct the reader to fuller discussions of these matters. For the most part, I have focused attention on interpretation and criticism of the major works, drawing freely from the many studies published on individual poems. I have tried diligently to record my sources and borrowings; but after many years of reading it is difficult, if not impossible, to know whether an opinion is one's own or may possibly have been absorbed through one's reading years ago.

In addition to expressing gratitude and respect to those scholars who have written on Pope, to whom my debt is large, I also wish to thank my colleagues, Professors Edward H. Weatherly, William M. Jones, Dick A. Renner and Leon T. Dickinson, for their reading of the manuscript and for their helpful suggestions. I also want to express my gratefulness to Doctors John C. Tinsley, Jr. and Roland P. Ladenson, without whose help the completion of this book would have been impossible.

DONALD B. CLARK

University of Missouri
Columbia, Missouri

Contents

Chronology

1688   Alexander Pope was born on May 21 in London, the son of Alexander Pope, Sr., a linen merchant, and his second wife, Editha Turner. Both parents were Roman Catholic; and, possibly because of the anti-Catholic bias of the Glorious Revolution, the poet's father retired from his business the year of his son's birth and invested his savings of about £10,000 in French holdings.

ca.
1696   Having been tutored at home by a priest named Banister, alias Tavener, Pope entered Twyford School near Winchester. Later, however, he was withdrawn from Twyford and enrolled in Thomas Deane's school in London; there he perhaps remained until the family moved from London.

ca.
1700   In 1698 the poet's father bought Whitehill House at Binfield in Windsor Forest, an area evidently tolerant of Catholics; two years later the family settled in the forest.

ca.
1705   Spence records that Pope's health suffered a breakdown from too much study about this time; this was, however, the first attack of tubercular infection which plagued Pope for the rest of his life and resulted in curvature of the spine, headaches, smallness of stature (four feet, six inches at full growth), and general frailty.

1709   Pope's first published work, "Pastorals," appeared in May in Tonson's *Poetical Miscellanies*.

1711   In May, the "Essay on Criticism" appeared and led to a meeting of the author with Addison, who introduced Pope into his group of young Whig protégés at Button's Coffeehouse. About this time he met the Blount sisters, Teresa and Martha, the latter of whom became a lifelong friend.

1712 Steele published Pope's poem "Messiah" in *Spectator* 378, and Lintot's *Miscellany* included the first version of "The Rape of the Lock." Pope met and soon became a close friend of the Tory group—Swift, Arbuthnot, Parnell, and Gay—who formed the Martinus Scriblerus Club.

1713 In March, "Windsor Forest" celebrated the Tory Peace Treaty of Utrecht. By the end of the year Pope was seeking subscriptions for his proposed translation of the *Iliad*.

1714 Pope issued his expanded version of the "Rape of the Lock" in March. He first met Henry St. John, Viscount Bolingbroke, during this year.

1715 The first four books of the *Iliad* appeared in February. Pope also met Lady Mary Wortley Montagu.

1716 The second volume of the *Iliad* appeared in March.

1717 Pope's only venture into drama, a farce called *Three Hours after Marriage* and written in collaboration with Gay and Arbuthnot, was first acted in January. In June, the third volume of the *Iliad* came out, and Pope's first collected *Works* was offered to the public. Pope's father died on October 23.

1718 In June, the fourth volume of the *Iliad* was issued. With the income from the successful translation, Pope leased the villa of Twickenham on the Thames, near Richmond, and moved there with his mother.

1720 The last two volumes of the *Iliad* were published in May.

1721 Pope's edition of Thomas Parnell's *Poems* was published in December.

1723 In January, Pope's edition of the *Works* of John Sheffield, Duke of Buckingham, appeared, only to be confiscated by the government because the poet was suspected of sympathizing with the Jacobites.

1725 Pope's six-volume edition of Shakespeare's *Works* appeared in March. The next month the first three volumes of his translation of the *Odyssey* were published.

1726 Pope's edition of Shakespeare was attacked by Lewis Theobald, and in June the final three volumes of the *Odyssey* translation were published. Swift came over from Ireland and visited Pope.

1727 Swift again visited Pope, and in June they issued the first two volumes of the Pope-Swift *Miscellanies*. Pope was busy working on the *Dunciad*, which had originally been a Scriblerus project.

1728 The last volume of the Pope-Swift *Miscellanies* was published in March. In May the first version of the *Dunciad* in three books appeared. Pope's greatest efforts were to appear from now until the end of his career.

1729 The *Dunciad Variorum* was published in April.

1731 About 1730 Pope conceived of writing a series of poems which would comprise an ethical system. In December he published the first poem of the projected system, "Epistle to the Earl of Burlington, Of Taste." The public reception of the poem was unfavorable, and Pope feared that the whole enterprise might be jeopardized.

1733 To save his projected ethical system, Pope maneuvered the publication of his poems. In January he published under his own name the "Epistle to Bathurst," following it in February with the "First Satire of the Second Book of Horace Imitated, to Mr. Fortescue." He was willing to sacrifice these two poems—to allow them to draw the fire of his enemies—so that the major work, "An Essay on Man," to be published anonymously at the same time, might be spared. The ruse worked, and "An Essay on Man" was widely hailed; in a few years its authorship became known.

1734 In January, the "Epistle to Cobham" appeared, followed in the same month by the fourth epistle of "An Essay on Man," still under the guise of anonymity. Two lesser Horatian satires were also published.

1735 Pope's good friend Dr. John Arbuthnot was dying, and as a tribute to him Pope published the "Epistle to Dr. Arbuthnot" in January. The following month "To a Lady," the last of the "Ethic Epistles," appeared. In April, the second volume of Pope's collected *Works* came from the press to companion the first volume of 1717. In May, the unscrupulous publisher Edmund Curll offered the public an unauthorized edition of Pope's *Letters*.

1737 In April, "The Second Epistle of the Second Book of

Horace Imitated" appeared. For some time Pope had been concerned with immorality and corruption in the government controlled by Sir Robert Walpole, the Whig leader, who remained in office at least partly because of the support of George II and strong influences at the court. To call attention to the royal influence, Pope published "The First Epistle of the Second Book of Horace: To Augustus," an ironic attack on George II's indifference to things intellectual and cultural. Also in May, Pope's edition of his *Letters* was published to correct the wrong implications created by Curll's collection. A storm of criticism broke about Pope's head concerning the religious views expressed in the "Essay on Man," now acknowledged to be Pope's.

1738   Pope's concern over the state of English life and government expressed itself in four satiric utterances during the year: "The Sixth Epistle of the First Book of Horace, Imitated"; "The First Epistle of the First Book of Horace, Imitated"; "One Thousand Seven Hundred and Thirty Eight. A dialogue Something like Horace"; "One Thousand Seven Hundred and Thirty Eight. Dialogue Two." William Warburton, a clergyman, defended "An Essay on Man." Pope met Warburton later, in 1740.

1741   Pope published the *Memoirs of Martinus Scriblerus* and his correspondence with Swift, whom he had not seen since 1727. He and Warburton worked on a new version of the "Dunciad."

1742   In March their efforts produced the fourth book of that work, "The New Dunciad: As it was Found in the Year 1741."

1743   The final form of this poem appeared in October as "The Dunciad In Four Books Printed according to the Complete Copy found in the Year 1742."

1744   Pope had always liked to tinker with his poems and had revised almost every one in each successive edition of his *Works;* it is not strange, then, that he spent the last months of his life revising his total work for publication with Warburton's notes and explanations. He succeeded in publishing the "Essay on Criticism," the "Essay on Man," and the four "Ethic Epistles" ["Moral Essays"] before his death; the remainder of his work had to wait for Warburton's edition in 1751. On May 30, after receiving the last rites of the Catholic church, Pope died, from asthma and dropsy.

CHAPTER 1

The "Painted Mistress" and the "Purling Stream"

TOWARD the close of his life Alexander Pope cast a backward glance at his early poetry and described it in the following words:

> Soft were my Numbers, who could take offence
> While pure Description held the place of Sense?
> Like gentle *Fanny's* was my flow'ry Theme,
> A painted Mistress, or a purling Stream.
> ("Epistle to Dr. Arbuthnot," ll. 147–50)

Most commentators on Pope have accepted the distinction which he makes in this statement between his juvenile and mature work and have drawn the line at the publication in 1717 of the first collected *Works*.[1] In one way the distinction between "Description" and "Sense" is not entirely valid: Pope's early work was never "juvenile." From the very beginning his verse was mature in its insight into human nature, and it was moral in that it dealt with the problem of good and evil in society. In another way, however, the distinction is valid since in his early poems Pope was feeling his way by experimenting with verse traditions, through imitation and translation.

Pope was wise enough to destroy his true "juvenilia." What we know about those earliest efforts comes from Joseph Spence's "conversations" with Pope:

I began writing verses of my own invention, farther back than I can well remember.—Ogilby's translation of Homer was one of the first large poems that ever Mr. Pope read; and he still spoke of the pleasure it then gave him, with a sort of rapture, only in reflecting on it.—"It was that great edition with pictures, I was then about eight years old. This led me to Sandy's [*sic*] Ovid, which I liked extremely; and so I did a translation of part of Statius, by some very bad hand."—P.

When I was about twelve, I wrote a kind of play, which I got to be acted by my schoolfellows. It was a number of speeches from the Iliad; tacked together with verses of my own.—The epic poem which I began a little after I was twelve, was Alcander, Prince of Rhodes: there was an under-water scene in the first book, it was in the Archipelago.—I wrote four books toward it, of about a thousand verses each; and had the copy by me, till I burnt it, by the advice of the Bishop of Rochester, a little before he went abroad.—P.

I endeavoured, (said he, smiling), in this poem, to collect all the beauties of the great epic writers into one piece: there was Milton's style in one part, and Cowley's in another; here the style of Spenser imitated, and there of Statius; here Homer and Virgil, and there Ovid and Claudian.—"It was an imitative poem, then, as your other exercises were imitations of this or that story?"—Just that.—P.[2]

From this record one learns of Pope's interest in "imitation" of various genres: the epic tradition, and by implication, that of the pastoral (Virgil, Spenser, and Milton) and that of the Ovidian elegy and heroic epistle. Pope was not destined to write an epic, but he so steeped himself in the tradition of the form that not only do many of his poems reflect verbal echoes from the *Iliad,* the *Odyssey,* and *Paradise Lost,* but he was also able to put this knowledge to good use when he wrote the greatest mock epic in the English language. Moreover, he was eventually to produce the best translation of the *Iliad* and *Odyssey* in his century.

The general concept of "imitation," alluded to in the conversations quoted from Spence, was to be a basic characteristic of Pope's total work, from the early attempts to reproduce Chaucer for his own day through the Horatian "Imitations" to the final version of the *Dunciad.* There is a unity throughout. Thus, Pope's early experimentation, or "pure Description," was to flower into the poetry of "Sense," a later poetry which would differ from the earlier not so much in kind as in degree. The earlier experimentation was the seed so planted and cultivated that the later harvest might be more abundant.

The first poem Pope published was written in the pastoral tradition. This form was a good one for a young beginning poet: it was a short form to sustain; its antecedents stretched far back into the Classical past of Greece and Rome, where it had been honored by the poets Theocritus, Bion, Moschus, and Virgil; and it was a popular form in Pope's day because the tradition had been kept alive by Spenser and Milton and by Dryden's translations. Moreover, it was held in high esteem by Pope's new friend, William Walsh, who along with William Congreve, William Wycherley, George Granville, and Henry Cromwell formed the first group of literary men to express interest in the young poet. They had been friends of Dryden in the days of the Restoration and knew well the niceties of poetic theory and practice.

Throughout his life Pope seemed to need friends who could discuss his work with him and advise him. The first of these had been William Wycherley. The circumstances of their meeting are not known, but by 1705 they were friends despite the disparity in their ages. Although the friendship was severely strained about 1710 when Pope, at Wycherley's request, tried to help the older poet revise his verses, it lasted until Wycherley's death in 1716. There is no evidence that Wycherley helped Pope with his writing.

This is not true, however, with Pope's second friend, William Walsh. Walsh was a country squire, a gallant, a wit, a rake, a friend to the great, a poet, and a member of the House of Commons. Dryden had said that Walsh was "without flattery, the best critic of our Nation." Walsh, having read some of Pope's "Pastorals" and the Preface which explains their principles, wrote Wycherley on April 20, 1705, asking his old friend to introduce him to Pope.[3] The five extant letters which then passed between Walsh and Pope in 1706 deal mainly with principles of pastoral poetry and drama and with Walsh's desire to see Pope continue working in the genre. Walsh showed one of the "Pastorals" to the publisher Jacob Tonson, who, on April 20, 1706, requested Pope's permission to publish the poem.

I *"Pastorals"*

Although it was his first poem to be solicited, Pope did not allow the "Pastorals" to appear until Tonson's *Poetical Miscellanies, the Sixth Part*, came out in 1709. This delay was doubtless caused by the young author's constant revisions of the four poems, a practice which may have resulted from Walsh's advice to make "correctness" his study and aim. Certainly Pope's manuscript is filled with corrections in Walsh's handwriting. It is more likely that Pope wanted his first printed effort to be perfect. He later told

Spence, "There is scarce any work of mine in which the versification was more laboured than in my Pastorals." [4]

The four "Pastorals" follow the four seasons of the year, and with this cyclic structure Pope establishes the order of nature as a theme; and time, or mutability, as a complementary theme. The time sequence is also developed by the setting of each pastoral at a different period of the day: early morning ("Spring"), mid-day ("Summer"), sunset ("Autumn"), and moonlight ("Winter"). [5] The central theme of order in nature can be seen in Pope's treatment of man in terms of the old philosophic system of correspondences between nature and man. Nature shares man's feelings of happiness and grief; it shares his experience of death and transfiguration; what affects the one moves the other. Such a view of the intimate relationship of man and nature is particularly suited to the pastoral poem because it symbolizes through its stylized settings the Age of Gold—that early period of man's history when he was still innocent in a world of uncorrupted nature. There man was the ideal shepherd—simple, innocent, heroic—the inheritor of the good and tranquil life in which man, beast, and the deities of nature communicated freely.

"Summer" presents this Virgilian scene more obviously than the other three "Pastorals," but it is evident in all four. "Spring," which is addressed to Sir William Trumbull (a childhood friend), derives from Virgil's seventh "Eclogue" and is cast in the form of a singing contest between two shepherds. A melancholy love complaint, "Summer" is dedicated to Pope's friend Dr. Garth and loosely follows the eleventh "Idyll" of Theocritus, Virgil's second "Eclogue," and Spenser's "Shepherd's Calendar." "Autumn," another song contest, patterned after Virgil's sixth "Eclogue," honors William Wycherley; and "Winter," an elegy in memory of a dead shepherdess (Mrs. Tempest), is indebted to the first "Idyll" of Theocritus and to the fifth "Eclogue" of Virgil. Inasmuch as Walsh had asked Pope to dedicate a poem to the memory of his friend Mrs. Tempest and since he himself died two weeks before its appearance, "Winter" in reality memorializes Walsh.

Unfortunately, the publication of the "Pastorals" embroiled Pope in his first literary quarrel. Six pastorals of Ambrose Philips had been published in Tonson's *Miscellanies* with the four of Pope, and the two groups of poems represented opposite points of view concerning pastoral theory. Pope, as his "Discourse on Pastoral Poetry" was to show when it was eventually published in 1717, stood firmly in the "neo-classic" tradition[6] which descended from Virgil to René Rapin, a French critic who codified the pastoral "rules" in an essay translated into English by Thomas Creech in 1684 as *Rapin's Discourse of Pastorals*. Rapin's views were shared by Walsh, Dryden, and Pope. This "neo-classic" theory contended that the pastoral should imitate the simplicity, innocence, and tranquillity of the Golden Age. The theory thus not only derived from the Ancients but also tried to represent that nature from which the Ancients deduced their rules.

In opposition to this view, Philips followed the "rationalistic," or modern, theory as it had been enunciated by Fontenelle in his *Discours sur la nature de l'églogue* (1688): the pastoral simply represents rural life, making no attempt to symbolize the Golden Age. Philips' shepherds are native English rustics, who live in a realistic natural setting and speak an archaic language. Philips' pastorals were praised by Joseph Addison in *Spectator* 523 (October 30, 1712) in glowing terms:

If any are of opinion, that there is a necessity of admitting these classical legends into our serious compositions, in order to give them a more poetical turn, I would recommend to their consideration the Pastorals of Mr. Philips. One would have thought it impossible for this kind of poetry to have subsisted without fauns and satyrs, wood-nymphs and water-nymphs, with all the tribe of rural deities. But we see he has given a new life, and a more natural beauty, to this way of writing, by substituting in the place of these antiquated fables, the superstitious mythology which prevails among the shepherds of our own country.

Not content with praising Philips and ignoring Pope, Addison then says that for a "Christian author" to use pagan fables "would be downright puerility, and unpardonable in a poet that is past sixteen." Inasmuch as Pope had claimed that the "Pastorals" were written when he was sixteen, it is entirely possible that Addison was either jibing at his precosity or branding the poems as immature.

Pope remained silent under the implied criticism, perhaps because he felt it would be presumptuous to question the judgment of Addison, who was by 1712 a man of formidable literary prestige and critical stature. But when Thomas Tickell, another member of the Addison coterie, published a series of five essays in April of 1713 (*Guardian* nos. 22, 23, 28, 30, 32), in which he expanded the "modern" pastoral theory and set himself up as a literary critic, Pope could no longer be quiet. He wrote the now famous ironic essay in *Guardian* 40 (April 27, 1713), which derided Philips' pastorals. While some personal animosity against Addison and his friends may have had a part in the incident, at its base was Pope's firm stand on the side of the Ancients and his opposition to the Moderns. To the end of his life he maintained his position, not out of any unyielding respect for rules or theory, but because to him the Ancient position represented culture as opposed to anarchy, art instead of ingenuity, civilization in the place of chaos. Here, for the first of many times in his life, Pope attempted to roll back the threatening flood of a subjective art and taste.

II *Translation of Chaucer*

Along with the "Pastorals," the Poetical Miscellanies of 1709 contained Pope's "January and May," a translation of Chaucer's *Merchant's Tale.* Pope was undoubtedly following the lead of Dryden, who had enjoyed some success with his Chaucerian translations in the *Fables* of 1700. Although Pope based his version on the 1687 Speght edition of Chaucer, it is obvious that he also relied on Dryden's modernizations.

Translation of the Classics had been popular in England since the Renaissance, and the list of the English poets who contributed to this effort was illustrious: Marlowe, Chapman, Sandys, Dryden —in fact, the name of almost any poet from the Renaissance to Pope's time could be found among the translators. Pope evidently believed that translation was excellent poetic training because, before he was seventeen, he had turned into English "Vertumnus and Pomona" (1712), the "Fable of Dryope" (1717), and "Polyphemus and Acis" (1749) from Ovid's *Metamorphoses;* and from his *Heroical Epistles,* "Sappho to Phaon" (1712); the "First Book of Statius His Thebais" (1712), the "Speech of Sarpedon to Glaucus" from the *Iliad,* Book XII (1709); and the "Arrival of Ulysses in Ithaca" from the *Odyssey* (1713).

Perhaps intrigued by his attempts to translate Chaucer, Pope returned to him about 1712. This time he chose a more ambitious work, Chaucer's "Hous of Fame," which he published in 1715 as "The Temple of Fame." This poem, however, is an "imitation," not a translation. The idea for Pope's poem came from Chaucer, but the poem itself is original and represents an eighteenth-century point of view. Chaucer's poem had been a love poem, so the "Hous of Fame" consisted of a temple to Venus and two lesser temples to Fame and Rumor; Pope's poem does not concern itself with love, so Venus and her temple are excluded. Chaucer's temple was Gothic in architecture; Pope's is eighteenth-century Palladian. Chaucer's heroes were obscure contemporaneous writers; Pope, drawing on his knowledge of history, peoples his temple with the great names of Classical antiquity.[7] Both poems are allegorical, but the use of allegory differs: the speaker in Chaucer's dream is a participant; Pope's narrator is a spectator; and, after observing the unpredictable nature of the goddess Fame, he decides in the final passages of the poem that an enduring heavenly fame is to be preferred to a fleeting earthly one. The objectivity of Pope's narrator and his conclusion in favor of heavenly fame reminds one of Milton's "Lycidas," in which another young poet struggles with the problem of fame. In fact, Pope's debt to Milton in this poem may be a considerable one.

"The Temple of Fame" gives insight into Pope's attitude toward fame at the age of twenty-three; but more important is the fact that the poem shows a definite advance in the use of allusive materials. The poem abounds in echoes from Horace, Ovid, Virgil, and from Dryden's translations of those Latin poets. The "Pastorals" had borrowed themes and incidents from Virgil; the translations of Chaucer had retold the narrative in eighteenth-century idiom; but neither of these efforts had succeeded in creating the kind of poetry which eventually carve a niche for Pope in a Temple of Fame—that evaluative kind of poetry which by allusion from other poetic contexts gives Pope's immediate context a richness and a suggestiveness of texture, a metaphoric quality of contrast between what once was and no longer is, or what is and what should be. In "The Temple of Fame," Pope for the first time achieved the kind of "wit" which was to make him the greatest poet of the eighteenth century.

III *"Messiah"* and *"Windsor Forest"*

Because he had succeeded in wresting Chaucerian translation
into an original "imitation," Pope perhaps hoped to do the same
with the pastoral form which he had first mastered. Whatever his
reasons, he continued experimenting with it, adapting the tradition to more complex subject matter and purpose in "Messiah"
and in "Windsor Forest." Whether he succeeded in this attempt
in "Messiah" is doubtful,[8] but "Windsor Forest" presents a mature
poet, exultant in his command over subject matter, language, and
allusion.

"Messiah" was published anonymously in the *Spectator* (May
14, 1712), but Pope acknowledged authorshop a few months later. In it he follows Virgil's fourth "Eclogue." Because Virgil's
poem had foretold the coming of a child who would usher in the
Golden Age, the Middle Ages had interpreted it as a prophecy of
the birth of Christ. Pope accepts this interpretation; and, by inter-
lacing Virgil's ideas with passages from the Old Testament
prophet Isaiah, he turns the pastoral to a new purpose and adds a
complexity to the texture of his poem. "Messiah," however, is not
successful because the Virgilian element and that from Isaiah remain for the most part separate and unfused.

Rhetorically, the poem is excellent: an alexandrine at line eight
states the prophecy ("A *Virgin* shall conceive, a *Virgin* bear a
son!"); the second section presents the fulfillment of the prophecy
in a pastoral scene, the era of peace and justice on an earth where
nature has been transfigured. This middle section ends with another alexandrine at line eighty-four, and the final twenty-four
lines extend the vision of the Golden Age into the future, even to
the Millennium, as the final alexandrine of the poem states, "Thy
Realm for ever lasts! thy own *Messiah* reigns!" The rhetoric is
controlled at every point in the poem, rising as a crescendo
through the first two sections to a thundering climax in the short
final passage.

With "Windsor Forest" Pope approximates that perfection
which marks his mature art. Although the poem was not published
until March 7, 1713, a letter from the Reverend Ralph Bridges to
Sir William Trumbull states that a version of it existed as early as

1707. Pope himself dated the beginning of the poem to the year 1704. The early drafts of "Windsor Forest" were undoubtedly other attempts in the pastoral form, written while Pope was revising the four "Pastorals," which were eventually published in 1709. "Windsor Forest" was rewritten several times and finally recast to celebrate the peace which was to be ushered in by the signing of the Treaty of Utrecht on April 11, 1713. Pope dedicated the poem to his friend George Granville, a fellow poet and statesman, who had not only asked Pope to celebrate the coming peace but who had also helped negotiate the treaty.

Most critical comment on "Windsor Forest" has stressed the lack of unity in the poem. For example, Professor George Sherburn comments: "The poem, quite typically, falls into fragments and does not make a unit. Curiously enough the break between the Trumbull and the Granville sections of the poem is not clearly marked." [9] And Professor Wimsatt also accepts this traditional view, though with a word of caution: "It is an accepted (if far from complete, and perhaps not quite accurate) criticism of *Windsor Forest* to say that the landscape is a sylvan gallery for portraits of sportsman and statesman." [10] Reuben Brower,[11] while he is interested primarily in studying Pope's use of allusive material from Roman sources, also sees the poem as having two main parts: (1) a brief invocation and (2) a description of Windsor Forest with its garden scene, mythological figures, and literary history.

That this view of the poem, as being incoherent, has prevailed can be charged partly to Pope's own account of its creation. When he reissued "Windsor Forest" in *Works* (1736), he felt it necessary to include a note stating that "This poem was written at two different times: the first part of it which relates to the country, in the year 1704, at the same time with the Pastorals: the latter part was not added till the year 1710 [more accurately, 1713], in which it was publish'd." Maynard Mack was, perhaps the first to challenge the view that the poem lacked organic unity, although he does not develop the idea: "[Pope] has made Windsor Forest his symbol . . . that is to say, Eden. Like Eden, like the world, England contains all things, with an order in variety, an equilibrium of opposites, that the older poets recognized as a mark of the

Creator's hand wherever seen." [12] The editors of the *Twickenham Edition* retain the view that "Windsor Forest" is in two parts, but they see them as comprising the unity of the poem:

In a poem like *Windsor-Forest* one cannot expect, nor does one often find, purely descriptive scenes of nature: the setting of the poem is always offering its analogue to human experience. It is not simply that the poem offers one a scene from nature and then injects into it a moral or ethical prescription; the two elements are rather fused in the one act of perception, for the poet in this instance is discovering meanings inherent in nature, not adding one thing to another.

In the light of this view of nature it is irrelevant, and a complete misunderstanding of *Windsor-Forest,* to praise Pope for having written something called "pure pastoral" down to l. 290 of his poem, and then to scold him for having spoiled it all by adding a sycophantic political conclusion. As any close study of the poem will reveal, the early descriptions of the "nature" about Windsor are always reflecting the divine or human orders of existence: the first long verse paragraph, ll. 7–42, reflects not only the order and variety of a cosmos governed by God, but also the peace and plenty of a kingdom governed by a Stuart queen. Because the moral and political realms are implicit in the poem from its start, it is rather pointless to speak of them as being "added" at the end. [13]

This view is shared by Professor Earl Wasserman, who carries it to its ultimate conclusion in his essay on "Windsor Forest," [14] and establishes beyond any doubt the complex unity achieved by Pope in the poem.

"Windsor Forest," then, is a poem both retrospective and contemporary in reference. In the manner of Sir John Denham in *Cooper's Hill* Pope combines two kinds of poems: the pastoral, with its mythological figures, and the topographical-political. Both the pastoral and the contemporary topical traditions are suggested in the opening lines of the poem:

> The Groves of *Eden,* vanish'd now so long,
> Live in Description, and look green in Song:
> *These,* were my Breast inspir'd with equal Flame,
> Like them in Beauty, should be like in Fame.
> Here Hills and Vales, the Woodland and the Plain,
> Here Earth and Water seem to strive again,

> Not *Chaos*-like together crush'd and bruis'd,
> But as the World, harmoniously confus'd:
> Where Order in Variety we see,
> And where, tho' all things differ, all agree.   (ll. 7–16)

The forest is a symbol of England, of nature, and of the world—an Eden, where order reigns; and thus Virgil's Golden Age under Augustus can be Pope's under Queen Anne. It is orderly, because order "in Variety" is nature's plan, wherein contraries are "harmoniously confus'd" ("Hills and Vales," "Woodlands and Plain," "Earth and Water").

This view of nature as "Order in Variety" is based partly on the idea of the Chain of Being but more so on the Classical principle of *discordia concors*. The Great Chain of Being[15] can be found in the *Timaeus* of Plato, but the concept probably goes further back into the remote past. After Plato, Aristotle accepted the doctrine, as did the Hebraic scholars of Alexandria who developed the concept and passed it on to the medieval Scholastics; these in turn harmonized it with Christianity and then bequeathed it to the neo-Platonists. By Pope's day this idea was an accepted commonplace but was losing its force under the continued discoveries of science.

According to the concept of the Chain, nature was one vast system of interdependent "links," each dependent upon the one above and below it. At the top was God, the omnipotent creator. Below God were ranged in descending order the nine "links" of angels who comprised the spiritual or rational world: Seraphim, Cherubim, Thrones, Dominions, Virtues, Powers, Principalities, Archangels, and Angels. Man, possessing a rational soul, or spiritual nature, in common with the angels—as well as a material body in common with the lower half of creation—occupied the middle "link." Because of his dual nature and unique position in the system, man was often referred to as "the microcosm of the macrocosm." Beneath man fell the lower half of the Chain, the world of matter: the animal kingdom, the vegetable, and the mineral. At the very bottom was "nothingness," as at the top was God, or "totality."

In such a system each link provided "Variety"; but, because every link was related to every other link and all to God, there was "Order in Variety"; and the world was thus "harmoniously confus'd." But acting through the Chain of Being is the principle of "friendly discord," the *discordia concors:* the belief that the order of the universe results from God's reconciliation of contraries. This theory had been applied to the material universe by Heraclitus, Plato, Cicero, Ovid, and others; but it was adopted by Christianity to explain how God could produce good from evil. By the time of the Renaissance, the doctrine was used to explain politics, ethics, economics, and art. In these areas of knowledge, order or harmony is the central point between extremes.

"Windsor Forest" celebrates the signing of a peace treaty, the *discordia concors* between warring nations. The peace itself was a Tory victory, and *discordia concors* was the Tory view in politics inasmuch as the Whig revolution of 1688 had unbalanced the power between Parliament and the monarchy. Thus, the universal law of nature operates in nature (the forest), in the Treaty of Utrecht (peace), and in the political framework of the peace (the Tory political view).

By poetry Windsor Forest has been metamorphosed into a symbolic place, an idealized nature ("The Groves of Eden"). It is a description of a Golden Age which can be achieved in England and in the world, a metamorphosis which the Tory-minded Anne is bringing about through peace and commerce: "Rich Industry sits smiling on the Plain,/And Peace and Plenty tell, a Stuart reigns (ll. 41–42).

It is against this symbolic background that the incidents which occur in the poem should be seen:

> Not thus the Land appear'd in Ages past,
> A dreary Desert and a gloomy Waste,
> To savage Beasts and Savage Laws a Prey,
> And Kings more furious and severe than they:
> Who claim'd the Skies, dispeopled Air and Floods,
> The lonely Lords of empty Wilds and Woods.   (ll. 43–48)

Pope thus begins his historical (and symbolic) action in the days of William I, the Norman conqueror of England. This is the Iron Age of Virgil's *Georgics* contrasted to his Golden: the tyranny, savagery, and want in England under a foreign king contrasted to the "Peace," "Plenty," and "Liberty" of "Britannia's Goddess, [who] rears/Her chearful Head, and leads the golden Years" (ll. 91–92)—the Tory Anne.

In those dark and oppressive days William I ravaged the land that he might set aside another forest—the New Forest of Hampshire—as a royal hunting preserve. The imagery of the passage (ll. 43–78) emphasizes the idea that William's hunting was against God, nature, law, and man: tyranny prevailed, nature and man were ravaged, and hunting was a form of war. But this violation of nature's *discordia concors* was avenged by God. William Rufus, the son of William I, was slain during a hunt; and the death of William I himself was hastened by a hunting accident. Each became "At once the Chaser and at once the Prey" (l. 82). Since Pope has used hunting as a metaphor for tyranny, he is able to turn William I's hunting into a covert criticism of Whig King William III, who destroyed the political *discordia concors:* both bore the same name; both were foreigners; both died prematurely because of hunting accidents; both liked hunting in the sense that it was a form of war and they both used war as a political weapon; and both, from the Tory political point of view, were tyrants. The first hunting scene, then, not only symbolizes war— a blasphemy against God and nature—but also suggests that the Whig reluctance to sign the peace treaty is equally blasphemous.

In the second scene (ll. 93–158) the hunt is in accord with nature: man hunts in each of the seasons and in air, water, and on earth. Because the hunt takes place in the idealized Windsor Forest, it is an idealized or metamorphosed form of war—"The Youth rush eager to the Sylvan War" (l. 148). That Pope sees war transmuted into an ideal hunt is evident from his imagery, which identifies hunting with war. The hunters are compared with soldiers:

> Thus (if small Things we may with great compare)
> When *Albion* sends her eager Sons to War,
> Some thoughtless Town, with Ease and Plenty blest,
> Near, and more near, the closing Lines invest;
> Sudden they seize th' amaz'd, defenceless Prize,
> And high in Air *Britannia's* Standard flies.   (ll. 105–10)

The pheasant "feels the fiery Wound/Flutters in Blood, and panting beats the Ground" (ll. 113-14).

Whereas the first episode shows that man's activities produce discord and chaos because they are uncontrolled and against nature, the second episode, through contrast, pictures his endeavors as they should be: the norm of controlled activity in accord with nature. Such an accord is the true *discordia concors* between man and nature. This second kind of hunting in Windsor Forest is enjoyed by Queen Anne, who acts as a Diana of the woods:

> Let old *Arcadia* boast her ample Plain,
> Th'Immortal Huntress, and her Virgin Train;
> Nor envy *Windsor!* since thy Shades have seen
> As bright a Goddess, and as chast a Queen;
> Whose Care, like hers, protects the Sylvan Reign,
> The Earth's fair Light, and Empress of the Main.
> (ll. 159–64)

In contrast to Whig William III of the first scene, Queen Anne and her hunting suggest here the Tory political view: sign the peace treaty between the warring nations and turn England and the world into an idealized Windsor Forest, where man is one with nature.

The third hunting scene again treats this theme of metamorphosis, but in mythic rather than historical terms. Pope borrows the Pan-Syrinx story from Ovid to present his theme. Syrinx becomes Lodona, or the River Loddon, which flows into the Thames near Binfield. Lodona, hunting one day and "eager of the Chace," "Beyond the Forest's verdant Limits stray'd,/*Pan* saw and lov'd, and burning with Desire/Pursu'd her Flight; her Flight increas'd his Fire" (ll. 182–84). In terms of the poem's symbolism, the incident is again a violation of the *discordia concors*: Lodona is too active; and, in crossing the boundary of Windsor Forest, "Eden," she finds herself outside the protection of ordered nature; and, just as William I was punished for his violation of nature by the death of his sons, Lodona is punished: the hunter becomes the hunted.

Lodona's violation of the "friendly discord," however, is unlike that of William I. She is merely careless, not destructive of order. She prays to Diana for forgiveness and "melting as in Tears she lay/In a soft, silver Stream dissolv'd away" (ll. 203–4). Through her metamorphosis she combines within herself the active and the contemplative life—once again the *discordia concors*. Lodona thus introduces the next section of the poem—Sir William Trumbull's retirement from the active life of politics to the meditative life in the forest—with an account of the poets who lived in Windsor Forest and wrote of ordered nature. They represent the meditative side of life, just as the hunting episodes symbolized the active.

Metamorphosis is the key to the poem. As war is changed into hunting, as war is transmuted into peace, as Lodona was transformed into a river, so poetry transcends actual nature and presents a nature metamorphosed, perfected, and idealized—"the musing Shepherd spies/The headlong Mountains and the downward Skies" (ll. 211–12) in Lodona's smooth surface. Poetry presents nature as

> The Groves of *Eden*, vanish'd now so long
> Live in Description, and look green in Song;
> . . . .
> Here Earth and Water seem to strive again,
> Not *Chaos*-like together crush'd and bruis'd,
> But as the World, harmoniously confus'd:
> Where Order in Variety we see,
> And where, tho' all things differ, all agree.
> (ll. 7–8, 12–16)

"Windsor Forest" is Pope's early statement about the nature of poetry—as was Milton's "Lycidas," [16] whose fountain Arethusa was changed into a stream, and as was Marvell's "Garden," where "Pan did after Syrinx speed/Not as a nymph, but for a reed." So Pope lists only those Windsor poets who present such a poetic heightening of English kings (ll. 259–328) and history, a catalogue which ends with Anne in the act of imitating the divine fiat: "At length great ANNA said—Let Discord cease!/She said, the World obey'd, and all was *peace!*" (ll. 328–329). Anne's act of peace is in itself a metamorphosis of chaotic war into another kind of commerical war—trade; and the *discordia concors* is thus achieved. Since England's trade is dependent on shipping, the Thames River symbolizes the commerce. The Thames flows through Windsor Forest and beyond, even to the ends of the earth through the oceans. The river thus combines the reflective and the active life, and it is thus fitting that the vision of Father Thames, which closes the poem (ll. 329–422), presents the Golden Age of the world under Anne and Tory policy, a world where "The shady Empire shall retain no Trace/Of war or Blood, but in the Sylvan Chace" (ll. 371–72).

"Windsor Forest" brings to an end Pope's experimentation with the pastoral form and leaves the poet standing on the threshold of his mature work. He himself seemed aware of this. As Virgil had done before him, Pope closes "Windsor Forest" with the line "First in these Fields I sung the Sylvan Strains," a rewording in the past tense of the first line of "Spring," his first pastoral: "First in these Fields I try the Sylvan Strains." Pope was never again to use the pastoral to depict a possible Golden Age for mankind. In all his later work he used the pastoral Golden Age for satiric purposes to show how far man has fallen from the Eden which might have been his.

IV *"An Essay on Criticism"*

"Windsor Forest," then, brings to a close the first creative period of Pope's life which began in 1705 with the discussions of the pastoral with William Walsh. About the same time, and probably also under the influence of Walsh, Pope had begun work on a poem in a genre relatively new in English poetry—the essay. The poem underwent considerable revision for several years until it was finally published anonymously in May, 1711, as "An Essay on Criticism." The poet's most ambitious work up to that time, it consists of three parts; it deals with controversial subjects and critical issues, and it is cast into a literary form which had little tradition or precedent.[17]

The "Essay" provoked an almost immediate attack and a vitriolic critique by John Dennis in his *Reflections Critical and Satyrical, upon a late Rhapsody, call'd An Essay upon Criticism.* This abusive monograph was apparently written because of two couplets in Pope's poem:

> 'Twere well, might Criticks still this Freedom take;
> But *Appius* reddens at each Word you speak,
> And *stares, Tremendous!* with a *threatning Eye,*
> Like some *fierce Tyrant* in *Old Tapestry!*   (ll. 584–87)

Since Dennis' play *Appius and Virginia* had failed upon production in 1709, the crusty old critic took Pope's lines to refer to himself and evidently felt they were an attempt to discredit his critical position. Dennis, a follower of the rationalistic school of
Thomas Rymer, possessed formidable stature; and there can be
little doubt that Pope's less rigorous position on the "rules" in the
Essay would be anathema to him. Although Pope had published
the poem anonymously, Dennis suspected its authorship; and,
being a Protestant supporter of William III, he attacked the anonymous author as a Jacobite and a Catholic.

The Essay has been one of Pope's most popular as well as controversial poems. The reasons for the controversy engendered are
not only the debatable issues involved in its subject matter but
also the deliberate ambiguity of Pope's critical position. In the
"Essay" Pope is much closer to Dryden's position than to that of
the Rymer-Dennis school, and Dryden is often charged with in-
consistency in his critical writings. Dennis leveled the same charge
at Pope. But, whereas Dryden changed his views on certain critical
matters, Pope maintains a consistent principle throughout the
essay; indeed, his theory of poetry in the "Essay on Criticism" is
at one with his total theory and practice of poetry throughout his
career. Pope suspends his theory, maintains it in an ambiguous
position, or in "friendly discord," between the apparent opposition
of "wit" and "judgment," "art" and "nature," "rules" and "nameless graces."

In Part I of the "Essay on Criticism," which discusses the general and philosophic bases on which a critic can make sound judgments, Pope advises,

> Those RULES of old *discover'd*, not *devis'd,*
> Are *Nature* still, but *Nature Methodiz'd;*
> *Nature,* like Liberty, is but restrain'd
> By the same Laws which first *herself* ordain'd.
> . . . .
> Learn hence for Ancient *Rules* a just Esteem;
> To copy *Nature* is to copy *Them.*   (ll. 88–91, 139–40)

But along with such advice Pope also warns,

> Some Beauties yet, no Precepts can declare,
> For there's a *Happiness* as well as *Care.*

> *Musick* resembles *Poetry,* in each
> Are *nameless Graces* which no Methods teach,
> And which a *Master-Hand* alone can reach.
> If, where the *Rules* not far enough extend,
> (Since Rules were made but to promote their End)
> Some Lucky Licence answers to the full
> Th' Intent propos'd, *that Licence* is a *Rule.*   (ll. 141–49)

The seeming contradiction is only on the surface. The rules may be based on reason and may reflect the order and regularity of nature, but within the harmony of nature there is also room for variety—irregularity, or the "nameless graces," the *je ne sais quoi,* which only genius can produce and "taste." Thus, a theory of poetry should be a golden mean between the objective rules, which produce correctness, and the intuitive principle of genius and taste, which allow for individual differences in poets and critics.

Again, the ostensible antithesis of "art" and "nature" is not an actual dichotomy in Pope's theory. He could safely assume that his readers understood what he meant by nature, and so he does not define it. The most quoted lines in the "Essay" state his concept of imitation: art imitates nature, a thesis practically axiomatic in Western civilization since the eras of Plato and Aristotle, as Pope implies in Part III when he surveys the critical tradition:

> First follow NATURE, and your Judgment frame
> By her just Standard, which is still the same:
> *Unerring Nature,* still divinely bright,
> One *clear, unchang'd,* and *Universal* Light,
> Life, Force, and Beauty, must to all impart,
> At once the *Source,* and *End,* and *Test* of *Art.*
> *Art* from that Fund each *just Supply* provides,
> Works *without Show,* and *without Pomp* presides:
> In some fair Body thus th' informing Soul
> With Spirits feeds, with Vigour fills the whole,
> Each Motion guides, and ev'ry Nerve sustains;
> *It self unseen,* but in th' *Effects,* remains.   (ll. 68–79)

Pope and his age inherited their view of nature from the Renaissance critics, particularly from the Italian commentators on Aristotle's *Poetics* and on Horace's *Ars Poetica.* The work of these

[32]

critics, in turn, had been recast by the French seventeenth-century critic Boileau, to whom Pope pays homage. Nature reflects in its order and regularity the harmony and order of its Creator, God. Man, created in the image of God, can perceive this universal order. Man's faculty of reason feels a kinship with the Creator, who is "total reason." Thus in imitating "unerring Nature," art should present this divine orderliness and harmony of nature. It does so by presenting a kind of truth which is objective and universal rather than subjective and specific. Such truth, when checked by the faculty of reason, will be found to be approximately the same in all ages in all educated, intelligent individuals; and in imitating this truth, art will present a nature which is ideal as well as normative. While it is true in nature that an occasional two-headed calf is born, such an aberration is not the proper nature for art to imitate. It is not normative, it is specific; it is not the universal pattern for calves. The nature which art imitates should be generic.

The judgments of men, however, differ; and, because they do, men may interpret even universal nature in differing ways. It is here that the "rules" help check the idiosyncrasies and individual differences in men's judgments. The "rules" represent a kind of secondary imitation, or are at least guides, which channel and restrict the subjectivity of the artist and keep him closer to nature:

> Those RULES of old *discover'd*, not *devis'd*
> Are *Nature* still, but *Nature Methodiz'd*:
>
> . . . .
>
> Hear how learn'd *Greece* her useful Rules indites,
> When to repress, and when indulge our Flights.
> (ll. 88–89; 92–93)

The Italian and French Renaissance critics eventually reduced these ancient principles of nature into the "rules" which became inviolate laws to such strict critics as Rymer and Dennis. Even to less rigid critics, like Pope, the rules were helpful in charting the course for the poet. By following the rules one would, in a sense, be following nature, since the ancients followed nature, and the rules codified their practice:

> When first young *Maro* in his boundless Mind
> A Work t' outlast Immortal *Rome* design'd,

> Perhaps he seem'd *above* the Critick's Law,
> And but from *Nature's Fountains* scorn'd to draw:
> But when t' examine ev'ry Part he came,
> *Nature* and *Homer* were, he found, the *same:*
> Convinc'd, amaz'd, he checks the bold Design,
> And Rules as strict his labour'd Work confine,
> As if the *Stagyrite* o'erlook'd each Line.
> Learn hence for Ancient *Rules* a just Esteem;
> To copy *Nature* is to copy *Them.*   (ll. 130–40)

But always, the "rules," which parallel "art," must be kept in accord with the "nameless graces," or nature. True art results from both, not from one alone.

The same necessity for maintaining a mean can be seen in Pope's treatment of "wit" and "judgment."[18] Professor George Sherburn gives a useful definition of "wit" by distinguishing it from "nature": "Nature as the universe, 'the scale of Being,' is the material source of all art; while Wit, though very commonly meaning material proper for use in literature, tends to mean material that has passed through the mind of the artist."[19] The word "wit" was in a state of transition in Pope's day; and, although he uses it forty-six times in the "Essay on Criticism"—often with different meanings, which range the spectrum from the older Elizabethan term for "native intelligence" to our modern synonym for "humor"—in general all its meanings are related to Professor Sherburn's basic definition. "True wit" would follow nature and produce a work of art having nature's order in it; "false wit" would produce empty ingenuity. Pope has the latter kind in mind as he remarks,

> Some, to whom Heav'n in Wit has been profuse,
> Want as much more, to turn it to its use;
> For *Wit* and *Judgment* often are at strife,
> Tho' meant each other's Aid, like *Man* and *Wife.*
> 'Tis more to *guide* than *spur* the Muse's Steed;
> Restrain his Fury, than provoke his Speed;
> The winged Courser, like a gen'rous Horse,
> Shows most true Mettle, when you *check* his Course.
> (ll. 80–87)

It is obvious from Pope's image of the husband and wife that he expects "true wit" to live in "friendly discord" with "judgment."

Both must give of their rights in order to produce the best results in creating poetry or criticizing it. This theme Professor Maynard Mack in another context calls "constructive renunciation":

One way of stating this, as we have seen, would be to call it the theme of constructive renunciation. By renouncing the exterior false Paradises the true one within is won; by acknowledging his weaknesses man learns his strengths; by subordinating himself to the whole he finds his real importance in it. Renunciation in this sense, conceived not as stagnation of the spirit but redirection toward its truest ends, is a ruling principle with Pope. It appears in the *Essay on Criticism*, where it is the foundation of all the qualifications specified for critics: we excel by giving up—not only what is inappropriate to the individual self but what is inappropriate to man as man.[20]

When Pope writes that

> *True Wit* is *Nature* to Advantage drest,
> What oft was *Thought*, but ne'er so well *Exprest*,
> *Something*, whose Truth convinc'd at Sight we find,
> That gives us back the Image of our Mind,   (ll. 297–300)

he is stating the complementary relationship between "wit" and "judgment." "Judgment," like nature, is the material, the subject, of art—the sound knowledge and the intellectual part of it. Wit, however, as Edward Hooker has pointed out, was a "special way of thinking, peculiar to literature," just as the rational method was to mathematics. "Wit possessed unique values" because it "provides an insight into nature ['by revealing hidden relationships'], endows it with 'Life, force, and beauty,' and conveys it directly to our hearts, charming us as it makes us wiser." [21]

Part I of the "Essay on Criticism" thus treats of essentials—truths basic to both poets and critics. Pope has been accused of confusing the poet and the critic in his "Essay," but he has not. Rather, he correctly sees that, if a critic is to make sound judgments on poetry, he must first understand the proper basis of art itself.

Having disposed of objective fundamentals in Part I, in Part II Pope turns his attention to personal qualities which could hinder true judgment in the critic. Just as Pride heads the list of the

Seven Deadly Sins, this characteristic in a critic is the worst of all
critical sins:

> Of all the Causes which conspire to blind
> Man's erring Judgment, and misguide the Mind,
> What the weak Head with strongest Byass rules,
> Is *Pride,* the *never-failing Vice of Fools.*
>
> . . . .
>
> Pride, where Wit fails, steps in to our Defence,
> And fills up all the *mighty Void* of Sense!
> (ll. 201–4, 209–10)

Just as pride can be the most subtle of the sins that separate man
from a true understanding of God, it can stand between the critic
and nature, reason, or judgment. The injection of pride into the
poem creates a moral overtone which, at times explicit, is always
implicit throughout the "Essay." The Augustans, inheriting the
Renaissance system of correspondences between human and inan-
imate nature, saw pride as a sin against God in any realm—moral,
intellectual, literary, or critical. The mention of any one plane
called into response metaphorically all other planes of correspondence. Thus the sin of pride in a critic corresponded to the
sin of not "following Nature" (in art); to not staying in one's place
in the "Chain of Being" (in the realm of morals and ethics); and
to not studying true knowledge (in learning).[22]

The other faults in critics enumerated in the rest of Part II
spring from pride in one realm or another: imperfect learning;
judging by parts of a poem, not by the whole; partiality to ancients or moderns; prejudice; singularity (individualism); incon-
stancy; political bias; and envy—a fault which cannot be dissoci-
ated from the province of morals. As Mr. Fenner points out, pride,
which at the beginning of Part II was a critical fault, has, by the
end, become a moral vice; and this shift in meaning effects the
transition to Part III, which opens with the line, "Learn then what
Moral Criticks ought to show" (l. 560).

The third section continues with a list of the good qualities a
critic should possess, most of them impinging on moral virtues:
candor, modesty, sincerity, good breeding, and freedom of advice.
This listing is climaxed by a character-sketch of the ideal critic
(ll. 631–42), who is also the good man; and Pope thus espouses

that Renaissance doctrine enunciated by Boccaccio, Minturno, and Milton. The ideal critic, though, is a man of the past: "Such once were *Criticks*, such the Happy *Few,/Athens* and *Rome* in better Ages knew" (ll. 643–44). And with these halcyon days Pope begins his survey of the history of criticism, in which he lists the great and near-ideal critics who transmitted culture and civilization down to his own day: Aristotle, Horace, Quintilian, Longinus, Erasmus, Vida, Boileau, Roscommon, and finally, William Walsh, the friend who had encouraged him to write.

That Pope lavished care and attention on the "Essay" is obvious from the fact that the modern reader is familiar with more quotations from it than from any other of Pope's poems. The "Essay" is not only Pope's first attempt to write outside a traditional genre, but it also marks his entrance into the territory of satire, a province over which he will eventually become the undisputed ruler; it is also his first attack on "dullness," and the cudgels caught from Dryden's hands were later used victoriously in the "Dunciad." In addition, the poem is his first statement in the raging controversy over the superiority of ancient versus modern literature; and, since its publication predates that of "Windsor Forest," "The Essay on Criticism," in its reconciliation of opposing critical principles, is Pope's first statement or at least foreshadowing of the principle of *discordia concors* so prominent in "Windsor Forest."

The success of the "Essay on Criticism" introduced Pope into a circle of new friends. In the early days of his life after his father had moved in 1700 to Binfield, Pope's acquaintances there were distinguished men but were not interested primarily in literature: Sir William Trumbull, The Reverend Ralph Bridges, John Caryll, and Martha and Teresa Blount. These Binfield friends introduced him to a few literary figures, relics of the Restoration, who had been associates of Dryden: Wycherley, Walsh, the actor Thomas Betterton, William Congreve, Henry Cromwell, Sir Samuel Garth, and George Granville, Lord Lansdowne. Shortly after the publication of the "Essay on Criticism" (1711), most of these men, except Garth and Congreve, were either dead or no longer on intimate terms with Pope. Meanwhile, Pope had met Richard Steele prior to 1711; and, when Addison praised the "Essay on Criticism" in *Spectator* 253 (December, 1711), Pope swung into the orbit of these two journalists.

The new friendship was at best built on shifting sands. Addison and Steele were partisan Whigs; Pope, a Roman Catholic, favored the Tory party. The real difficulty, however, lay in the circle of literary dilettantes who had attached themselves to Addison in his rise to prominence. Doubtless Addison enjoyed their adulation, for he encouraged their cliquishness by establishing in 1712 Button's Coffee-House, where they met to criticize one another's work and to hear the wisdom of their master, Addison. This "little Senate" counted among its members Ambrose Philips, Eustace Budgell, Thomas Tickell, John Hughes, Leonard Welsted, Charles Johnson, Henry Carey, and Henry Davenant. Pope probably did not know that Addison's work required him to enlist promising young writers in the Whig cause.

A few months later, under the aegis of Steele, Pope published the "Messiah" in the *Spectator* for May 14, 1712. He also wrote an undetermined number of *Spectator* essays; and, when the famous periodical resumed publication as the *Guardian* on March 12, 1713, Pope, assistant to Steele in the project, contributed numbers 4, 11, 40, 61, 78, 91, 92, and 173. In April, 1713, Pope offered a prologue for the production of Addison's tragedy, *Cato*. But Pope must have found his position almost untenable, torn between his older Catholic friends, the Whig coterie of Addison and Steele, and a new third circle of Tory friends: Swift, Parnell, Gay, and Arbuthnot.

The dissension became apparent when Addison's group began praising the "Pastorals" of Ambrose Philips over those of Pope in a series of five *Guardian* issues; these lauded Philips as the only successor to Theocritus, Virgil, and Spenser. Pope's eclogues were passed over without mention. Although the five papers were anonymous, it is likely that Tickell was their author. Doubtless Pope knew this; and, if one of the Button's group was the author, Addison, to Pope's mind, could hardly have been ignorant of the fact. Pope wrote an anonymous *Guardian* (No. 40) which purported to be the sixth essay in the series in praise of Philips' "Pastorals"; but a most cursory reading reveals it to be an ironic attack on this writer, who thereafter was to be known by posterity as "Namby-Pamby Philips." By the end of 1713 Addison had begun to manifest a coolness and reserve toward the younger poet. This aloofness was probably inspired by anonymous epigrams and gossip against Addison attributed to Pope.

A more important reason for the fading friendship with Addison, however, was Pope's new circle of friends, the Tory group of Jonathan Swift, Thomas Parnell, John Gay, and Dr. Arbuthnot. Swift, Arbuthnot, and Parnell were older than Pope and had known each other for some time; Pope and Gay were younger. Pope met Swift in the spring of 1713, probably through Parnell; and by the beginning of 1714 Pope had proposed to Swift and his friends that they issue a periodical entitled *Works of the Unlearned*, which was to satirize "all false taste in learning." Probably Pope intended the men to form only a loose literary association, but the group quickly evolved into the most famous and brilliant of all eighteenth-century social clubs—the Martinus Scriblerus Club. Soon Robert Harley, Earl of Oxford, and Francis Atterbury, Bishop of Rochester, joined the group. Although the club met only during the winter and spring of 1714, coming to an end with the death of Queen Anne and the rise of the Whigs to power, the members remained close friends; and over the next twenty years they occasionally turned their powers to satirical writings in the Scriblerian vein. If the proposed *Works of the Unlearned* was stillborn, other progeny of Martinus Scriblerus eventually entered the world in the form of individual pieces and collaborations.[23]

V *"The Rape of the Lock"*

There is little doubt that Pope, caught up in the spirit of new friends such as Swift and Gay, had little time or interest for Addison and his followers at Button's. Later in life, while reminiscing with Warburton about his relations with Addison, Pope thought there had been factors at work other than his preoccupation with the Scriblerus associates. One of these was Addison's behavior when Pope published his translation of the *Iliad;* the other concerned Pope's expansion of "The Rape of the Lock," which he had published in 1712 in Bernard Lintot's *Miscellaneous Poems and Translations* as a poem of three hundred and thirty-four lines in two cantos. When he decided to enlarge the poem he sought Addison's advice on the matter, with the following result, as related by Warburton; "he imagined [Addison] would have been equally delighted with the improvement. On the contrary, he had the mortification to have his friend receive it coldly; and more, to advise him against any alteration; for that the poem in its original state was a delicious little thing, and, as he expressed it, *merum sal.* Mr. Pope was shocked for his friend; and then first began to open his eyes to his Character." [24] Pope, remembering the "Pastorals" controversy, interpreted the advice as a result of jealousy on Addison's part. Ignoring Addison's advice he expanded and revised the poem to five cantos totaling 794 lines; and, since its publication in March of 1714, "The Rape of the Lock" has been his most popular and charming work.

The origin of this poem is one of the more intriguing anecdotes of literary history. In Binfield, Robert, Lord Petre, had cut off one of Arabella Fermor's curls. The incident led to an estragement between the two families. Pope's old friend John Caryll suggested to Pope that he write a poem to mollify them. Pope, who complied with Caryll's request and who later stated that he wrote the first version in less than two weeks in 1711, sent an advance copy to the persons involved; both seemed pleased. After publication, however, the two central figures changed their attitude, probably because friends who read the poem enjoyed its suggestive humor and could not refrain from comment and speculation. Pope's letters to Caryll throughout the year after the publication of the poem chronicle the poet's predicament,[25] which he eventually escaped when he dedicated the enlarged version of 1714 to Miss Fermor.

Perhaps the triviality of the incident between the Fermors and Petres suggested to Pope the mock-heroic genre as the proper one for such a poem; perhaps it was simply a desire to experiment further with poetic modes in these his formative years. Whatever the reason, Pope's choice could not have been happier. The mock-heroic possessed a long, worthy tradition. In English poetry Chaucer had written his "Nun's Priest's Tale," a fusion of the mock-heroic and the beast fable; but closer to Pope's own time stood Dryden's "MacFlecknoe," a scintillating gem of the type, but one flawed by lack of narrative and of supernatural machinery. Also, Pope's friend Sir Samuel Garth had published *The Dispensary* (1699), which was still enjoying an unprecedented success. Of greater significance, though, to Pope's poem were the writings of Nicholas Boileau, who expounded the principles of the mock-epic in *L'art Poetique* (1674) and practiced them in his *Le Lutrin* (1674–1683).

Unlike other mock-heroic poems in English, "The Rape of the Lock" achieves part of its perfection by its mockery of the complete epic—that is, every notable characteristic of the true epic is diminished in Pope's comic treatment. This was one of Boileau's theses. The very use of the epic form—ceremonious, grand, and dignified—to discuss a trivial or unworthy subject set up an ironic contrast which not only made possible laughter and comedy but also allowed for serious comment when desired. As Boileau describes the technique, all aspects of the epic may be mocked except its moral; thus, the mock-epic has a didactic function to perform. Pope's literary mockery manages to reduce innumerable epic traits. Among the more important are a feminine protagonist (for the epic hero); a card game (for the epic's battle); a pinch of snuff (for the epic's stratagem); the Cave of Spleen (for the epic's journey to the underworld); the Rosicrucian theory of the sylphs and gnomes (for the epic's encyclopedic tract of knowledge); the toilet scene (for the epic's arming of the hero); and the function of the sylphs and gnomes (for the epic's gods and goddesses who intervene in the action). The list could be continued down to minute details.[26]

Some characteristics of the epic Pope left untouched because they were the vehicle of serious social comment. For example, the Invocation to Caryll (ll. 1–6) is fraught with seriousness as well as gratitude to an old friend. The epic's Proposition is also followed by Pope with no hint of denigration:

> Say what strange Motive, Goddess! cou'd compel
> A well-bred *Lord* t' assault a gentle *Belle*?
> Oh say what stranger Cause, yet unexplor'd,
> Cou'd make a gentle *Belle* reject a *Lord*? (ll. 7–10)

This was necessary because the moral of the "Rape" arises from the theme of the poem, which is at least indirectly stated in the Proposition.

The metaphoric expression of this moral is an even greater fac-

tor in the perfection of the poem. If in the "Essay on Criticism"
Pope had written couplets, ones unforgettable because of their
precision and mastery of language, in the "Rape" he creates an
allusiveness which even his most mature work in later years could
not eclipse. One of Dryden's major devices of mockery in "Mac-
Flecknoe" had been to contrast the epic's high level of language
with a lower colloquial level in much the same way that he ironically juxtaposed his low hero, Thomas Shadwell, with figures of
high import, such as Christ, John the Baptist, Elijah, Hannibal,
and Aeneas. In contrast to Dryden's somewhat obvious method,
Pope achieves the same effect with much greater subtlety and literary sophistication by parodying the language of other great
poets and poems. The reader is made aware of the original context of a line parodied by Pope, and this context sets up an unseen
but not unheard ironic sounding board from which Pope's music
and meaning gain redoubled strength. Ariel's warning to the
lesser sylphs as he charges them with responsibility for Belinda's
care has often been praised for its beautiful tonal color and ono-
matopoeic effect:

> Whatever Spirit, careless of his Charge,
> His Post neglects, or leaves the Fair at large,
> Shall feel sharp Vengeance soon o'ertake his Sins,
> Be stopt in *Vials*, or transfixt with *Pins*;
> Or plung'd in Lakes of bitter *Washes* lie,
> Or wedg'd whole Ages in a *Bodkin*'s Eye:
> *Gums* and *Pomatums* shall his Flight restrain,
> While clog'd he beats his silken Wings in vain;
> Or Alom-*Stypticks* with contracting Power
> Shrink his thin essence like a rivell'd Flower.
> Or as *Ixion* fix'd, the Wretch shall feel
> The giddy Motion of the whirling Mill,
> In fumes of burning Chocolate shall glow,
> And tremble at the Sea that froths below!
> He spoke; the Spirits from the Sails descend;
> Some, Orb in Orb, around the Nymph extend,
> Some thrid the mazy ringlets of her Hair,
> Some hang upon the Pendants of her Ear;
> With beating Hearts the dire Event they wait,
> Anxious, and trembling for the Birth of Fate. (II, 123–42)

But lying beneath the surface of the lines are the Classical myth ("Ixion," l. 133), echoes from the *Iliad*, from Dryden's *State of Innocence*, and most of all from Milton's *Paradise Lost*, wherein Satan and the fallen angels welter in a lake of burning sulphur. In Pope's poem, Ariel threatens the sylphs with another kind of Hell: they will lie in puddles of spilled cosmetics and will burn in a "sea" of "burning Chocolate." In *Paradise Lost*, Book III, Satan journeys from planet to planet searching the newly-created universe for Earth; here, the sylphs descend "Orb in Orb" around Belinda, awaiting "With beating Hearts the dire Event/Anxious, and trembling for the Birth of Fate" (Belinda's falling in love) as heaven and earth awaited the Fall of Man in *Paradise Lost*. Despite the pleasure one derives from the witty use of such allusion and despite the laughter and humor produced by it, the allusions cannot completely dissociate themselves from their original context; thus, a darker atmosphere lies beneath the apparently sunny surface, ready to emerge and support serious comment when it is made.

It is through allusion and metaphor that Pope communicates his attitudes and feelings about the theme of the poem stated in the Proposition. The ostensible theme is the battle of the sexes, but the evaluation of human experience involved in this battle and its effect on the moral values of the society in which it is fought are conveyed through Pope's metaphoric language.

The action or plot of the "Rape of the Lock" provides little more than a dramatic situation about which Pope can weave his evaluation. Belinda awakens from a dream of beaux and gaiety on a fair, sunny day. She is attended by a cohort of sylphs, the spirits of departed coquettes, who are led by Ariel, her guardian sylph. Their function is outlined in the dream which Ariel whispers into Belinda's ear: [27]

> For when the Fair in all their Pride expire,
> To their first Elements their Souls retire:
> The Sprights of fiery Termagants in Flame
> Mount up, and take a *Salamander's* Name.
> Soft yielding Minds to Water glide away,
> And sip with Nymphs, their Elemental Tea.
> The graver Prude sinks downward to a *Gnome*,

In search of Mischief still on Earth to roam.
The light Coquettes in *Sylphs* aloft repair,
And sport and flutter in the Fields of Air.
    Know farther yet; Whoever fair and chaste
Rejects Mankind, is by some Sylph embrac'd:
For Spirits, freed from mortal Laws, with ease
Assume what Sexes and what Shapes they please.
What guards the Purity of melting Maids,
In Courtly Balls, and Midnight Masquerades,
Safe from the treach'rous Friend, the daring Spark,
The Glance by Day, the Whisper in the Dark;
When kind Occasion prompts their warm Desires,
When Musick softens, and when Dancing fires?
'Tis but their *Sylph*, the wise Celestials know,
Tho' *Honour* is the Word with Men below.   (I, 57–78)

In the dream passage Ariel also warns Belinda that this day will
be a fateful one:

In the clear Mirror of thy ruling *Star*
I saw, alas! some dread Event impend,
Ere to the Main this Morning Sun descend.
But Heav'n reveals not what, or how, or where:
Warn'd by thy *Sylph*, oh Pious Maid beware!
This to disclose is all thy Guardian can.
Beware of all, but most beware of Man!   (I, 108–14)

When Belinda awakens, she enhances her beauty with cosmetic
aids and then travels by boat down the Thames River to Hampton
Court, where she joins her social group. Here she flirts, accepts
the adulation of the men as her proper due, plays a game of cards
(symbolic of the battle of the sexes) and wins; but, as she presides over the tea table, the Baron, a suitor whom she favors in her
heart—thereby negating the influence of Ariel—cuts off one of her
two long curls. Belinda retires from the group to sulk (the Cave of
Spleen) and to worry about the loss of the curl. She asks a friend,
Sir Plume, to regain the curl from the Baron, but the Baron refuses. Utterly distraught by his refusal, Belinda becomes hysteri-
cal. Her friend Clarissa chides her and advises her to be practical,
but the advice only enrages Belinda, who now faces the Baron
and threatens him with a bodkin unless he return the curl. The

curl, however, has been translated to the sky; there it becomes a star to shine on future lovers and to confer immortality to the name of Belinda.

Upon this background of plot, slight and gossamer as it is, yet strong enough to support a parody of the epic, Pope, through metaphor and allusion, embroiders his tapestry of eighteenth-century morality. Into it he weaves the distortion and falsification of moral values wrought by the wrong aims and by the superficialities of his day. Any area of contemporary experience could have provided him with the material necessary to do this, but the particular circumstance which occasioned the "Rape of the Lock" determined its subject matter—the battle of the sexes. In order to show how the false standards, inherent in the battle, produce in turn hypocrisy and false morality in society, Pope depicts Belinda not only realistically as a much-sought-after, beautiful young woman but also as a symbol of the values desired in marriage in early eighteenth-century society. This symbolism becomes obvious in the toilet scene:

> And now, unveil'd, the *Toilet* stands display'd,
> Each silver Vase in mystic Order laid.
> First, rob'd in white, the Nymph intent adores
> With Head uncover'd, the Cosmetic Pow'rs.
> A heav'nly Image in the Glass Appears,
> To that she bends, to that her Eyes she rears;
> Th' inferior Priestess, at her Altar's side,
> Trembling, begins the sacred Rites of Pride.
> Unnumber'd Treasures ope at once, and here
> The various Off'rings of the World appear;
> From each she nicely culls with curious Toil,
> And decks the Goddess with the glitt'ring Spoil.
> This Casket *India's* glowing Gems unlocks,
> And all Arabia breathes from yonder Box.
> The Tortoise here and Elephant unite,
> Transform'd to *Combs*, the speckled and the white.
> Here files of Pins extend their shining Rows,
> Puffs, Powders, Patches, Bibles, Billet-doux.
> Now awful Beauty puts on all its Arms;
> The Fair each moment rises in her Charms,
> Repairs her Smiles, awakens ev'ry Grace,
> And calls forth all the Wonders of her Face;

Sees by Degrees a purer Blush arise,
And keener Lightnings quicken in her Eyes.
The busy *Sylphs* surround their darling Care;
These set the Head, and those divide the Hair,
Some fold the Sleeve, while others plait the Gown;
And *Betty's* prais'd for Labours not her own.   (I, 121–48)

The passage is an extended metaphor: Belinda is a goddess—at least she is so considered by her group—because of her beauty.[28] Her beauty is "awful," a word properly attributed only to deity. The process of the toilet to enhance beauty is analogous to a religious rite, as almost every line suggests—"mystic," "rob'd in white," "intent adores," "heav'nly Image," "bends . . . rears," "Altar's side," "sacred Rites," "awful Beauty." To strengthen the force of this extended metaphor, Pope further identifies Belinda with the sun, the source of light, life, and fertility in ancient myth and literary symbolism. Her eyes eclipse the sun (I, 13–14; II, 13–14) and have the power to destroy (I, 144; III, 155–56; V, 145–47); and her social system revolves around her, receiving its light and warmth from her as does the solar system from the sun. There are also slighter references to intensify her deity: as she begins the card game, she cries exultingly, "Let Spades be Trump! and Trumps they were" (III, 46) in parody of the *fiat lux*. She is waited upon by hosts of supernatural creatures, the sylphs. And in lines like "Belinda burns with more than mortal ire" (IV, 93) and "tempts once more thy sacrilegious Hands" (IV, 174), Pope suggests that to cut the lock of such a "divine" creature as Belinda is sacrilege.

Beauty, then, which has made a goddess of Belinda, is the paramount quality desired in woman. Beauty has replaced virtue; and, because society has elevated so superficial a thing, all moral values as a consequence are degraded. Chastity, a positive force for good, becomes negative in the mores of a society which holds such false values. Chastity is of no more significance than broken china—fragile, delicate, precious perhaps as an *objet d'art*, but replaceable. Three times in the poem Pope identifies the loss of chastity with the breaking of china (II, 105–6; III, 159–60; IV, 162–63). When society in its attitude toward marriage, so essential to society's very existence, substitutes the worship of beauty for true moral values, only hypocrisy can result. The appearance of virtue becomes more important than virtue itself. Belinda is more concerned about her reputation and appearance than about the actual lose of the symbolic curl (IV, 103–10, 171–76).

Another distortion of social and moral value can be seen in the downgrading of the male in a society which accepts appearance for reality. Not only does the poem mock the epic hero by presenting a feminine protagonist, but Pope three times yokes "Husbands" or 'Lovers" with "Lapdogs" (I, 15–16; III, 157–58: IV, 119–20). The implication is that they are equal in worth in a society which accepts a relative sense of value (the appearance: beauty) in the place of a true value (the reality: virtue).

This basic problem of appearance versus reality broods over the poem, and there is amidst the gaiety of "Fancy's Maze" always the serious moral indictment which creates a poignant sadness at marred beauty and at the human predicament itself. The passage dealing with Ariel's charge to the sylphs, cited above, hints at the Fall of Man. Certainly Belinda suffers a "fall." [29] The broken china imagery of the poem strongly suggests it. Moreover, Pope's use of allusion from *Paradise Lost* and the parody of his own translation of Sarpedon's speech from Book XII of the *Iliad* (published in *Poetical Miscellanies: the Sixth Part*, 1709), both of which form the very tissue and texture of the "Rape," almost insist upon the "fall" of Belinda. Professor Aubrey L. Williams points out three major parallels between Belinda and Eve: the dream of pride and vanity insinuated into Belinda's ear by Ariel (I, 27–114) and that into Eve's ear by Satan at the first temptation; Belinda's worshipping her own reflection in the mirror of her dressing table (I, 125–26) and Eve's first act after her creation—running to the nearby stream and admiring her reflection; and Ariel's retirement, "resign'd to Fate," when he finds an "earthly Lover lurking" in Belinda's heart (III, 143–46) and the hosts of angels who retire to heaven after the Fall of Adam and Eve.

Belinda's "fall" is not a literal loss of chastity. It is rather a fall from her chaste state of spirit, a mental state of virginity, preserved by the sylphs as long as she does not fall in love. By exercising her free choice and falling in love, Belinda has the means of escaping from her lack of fulfillment; but this possibility forces upon her yet another choice, the two alternatives of which are represented by the speeches of Thalestris (IV, 95–120) and Clarissa, whose remarks echo those of Sarpedon (V, 9–34). Thalestris urges revenge against man and proclaims female superiority. Clarissa (the Clarifier), however, advises the acceptance of reality with its true values. Reinforcing Clarissa's practical advice is the fact that her speech brings with it the weight of Sarpedon's noble remarks in their original context in the *Iliad*. Sarpedon, facing death, manifests such magnanimity of spirit that his defeat actually becomes his victory; from his "fall" he is able to rise to a more noble level of understanding. Clarissa's speech, then, suggests that Belinda may accept reality and thereby turn her loss into spiritual gain.

As Mr. Williams sums up the situation, "The only victory possible to Belinda is that victory which gallantry and generosity of spirit in the face of defeat or loss always gain, whatever the level of experience. Having fallen in love, Belinda has separated herself from the virginal purity symbolized by the sylphs, and she can then only be brave, keep good humor, and thus gain the support of a true and inner virtue, not the mere face of virtue." [30] Or, to put it into Professor Maynard Mack's terminology, it is the "theme of constructive renunciation," one already noted in the "Essay on Criticism." If Belinda is to mature into womanhood, she must sacrifice her lock; but for that sacrifice another kind of honor will recompense her loss. And so the tone moves from mockery to seriousness, from tenderness to sadness as Pope evaluates the changing dramatic situation which unfolds Belinda's conflict.

But Belinda is not able to resolve her discord. This inability is her true "fall," and through it Pope makes his most telling indictment of a society which predicates its most important convention on false premises. Not only do the allusions to Eve's fall in *Paradise Lost* and Sarpedon's speech imply this, but the Cave of Spleen episode underscores such an interpretation. Belinda's society has conditioned her attitudes, and she cannot transcend her own prudishness nor the false values of that society—the substitution of reputation (the appearance) for virtue (the reality). These false values become her Fate; unable to comprehend them and thereby to rise above them, she "falls."

Pope's choice of the mock-heroic to express the ambiguity and paradoxical nature of the human predicament—especially the situation of woman—could not have been improved upon. "The Rape of the Lock" is a perfect illustration of Professor Wasserman's exacting definition of neo-Classic art: "Neoclassic art is not the art of creating, but of inventing, or finding—the art of pursuing with perfect and unstrained consistency a system of similitudes inherent in the given materials." [31]

With the "Rape of the Lock" Pope reached that perfection toward which his experimentation had steadily led him. The "Essay on Criticism" and "Windsor Forest" had brought him far along on his journey to poethood, but with the "Rape" he reached his destination. Beyond the perfection he achieved in this poem he could not hope to go. Other journeys and destinations must be planned if he were to continue maturing as a poet, and it is doubtless with this self-knowledge in mind that he later interpreted this period of his development in the couplet, "That not in Fancy's Maze he wander'd long/But stooped to Truth, and moraliz'd his Song." [32] The poems produced during this first part of his creative work are more of "Fancy's Maze" than are the later satires. They are more experimental, imaginative, and fanciful. While it would be inaccurate to say that they do not deal with the actual world of men, they are not in a relative sense as specific and localized as the satirical poems. They present an idealized world in the "Pastorals," the "Messiah," and "Windsor Forest"; or a world which time has passed by in the Chaucerian translations; or the world of imaginative art in "The Temple of Fame," "Windsor Forest," and the "Rape of the Lock"; or a world of theory and precept rather than a world of practice in the "Essay on Criticism."

At the same time, these poems adumbrate the later Pope in their presentation of themes which will continue throughout his poetry; in their growing mastery over techniques of versification, which will make him the greatest poet of his century; and in their increasing fund of allusive material from other poets. This last technique established Pope as a poet who inherited the poetic traditions of English literature, and it enabled him to encompass in his work the past and the present simultaneously. The ten years which produced these early poems, while being formative, were probably the most important period of his creative life.

CHAPTER 2

The Interlude

WITH the unchallenged success of "The Rape of the Lock" in 1714, Pope had established himself as one of the leading poets of England. There are few recorded facts to explain why Pope devoted the next ten years of his life to translating and editing the works of others rather than creating new ones of his own. It seems fairly certain, however, that financial considerations determined his course. His statement to Spence is to that effect: "What led me into that [the translation of Homer], which was a work so much more laborious and less suited to my inclination, was purely the want of money. I had then none; not even to buy books." [1]

The paths of poetic glory might lead to fame, but they brought few of the things necessary to sustain a poet's life. Pope's family was not wealthy enough to continue supporting him while he wrote. As a matter of fact, when the first four books of the *Iliad* translation appeared in 1715 and were successful, the family sold its farm at Binfield and moved to a small house at Chiswick, just outside London. The move may be interpreted as indicating that the family was in financial difficulties and that Pope was now helping them. Moreover, Pope, a man of strong pride and independence, no doubt wanted to support himself, provided he could find a dependable source of income.

In casting about for a means of making money by his pen, Pope doubtless considered how previous poets had supplemented their small earnings from literary work. One of these means had been to translate the Classics into English, largely for the middle class, which was a new reading audience and unable to read the original Greek and Latin works. It was a respectable calling, as the greatness of the translators' names proved: Marlowe, Sylvester, Chapman, Dryden, and Addison among many. Pope had read translations from his youth; and, as he noted what had and had not been translated, he was undoubtedly aware that the last great translation of Homer, Chapman's version (1598–1616), no longer spoke to the English audience. Here was a task worthy the undertaking.

I *Translation of Homer*

Whatever his reasons may have been, Pope began talking about translating the *Iliad* in 1713; in October, he offered a subscription list. Addison encouraged him in the project. In May 1714, Pope republished the subscription offer; and the translation itself was soon under way in Binfield where Pope would be free from his friends and the distractions of London. Six months later, in November, he came to London to arrange for its publication. At this time he learned of Addison's duplicity in the matter. Since Addison had encouraged Pope to undertake the translation, Pope felt free to ask him to read his manuscript. Spence recounts Pope's version of the incident told to him some twenty years later:

There had been a coldness between Mr. Addison and me for some time, and we had not been in company together, for a good while, anywhere but at Button's coffee-house, where I used to see him almost every day.——On his meeting me there, one day in particular, he took me aside, and said he should be glad to dine with me in such a tavern, if I would stay till those people (Budgell and Philips) were gone. We went accordingly, and after dinner Mr. Addison said, "that he had wanted for some time to talk with me: that his friend Tickell, had formerly, whilst at Oxford, translated the first book of the Iliad. That he now designed to print it; and had desired him to look it over: he must, therefore, beg that I would not desire him to look over my first book, because, if he did, it would have the air of double dealing."——"I assured him that I did not at all take it ill of Mr. Tickell, that he was going to publish his translation; that he certainly had as much right to translate any author as myself: and that publishing both, was entering on a fair stage."—I then added, "that I would not desire him to look over my first book of the Iliad, because he had looked over Mr. Tickell's; but could wish to have the benefit of his observations on my second, I had then finished, and which Mr. Tickell had not touched upon." Accordingly, I sent him the second book next morning; and in a few days he returned it with very high commendation.——Soon after it was generally known that Mr. Tickell was publishing the first book of

CARNEGIE LIBRARY
LIVINGSTONE COLLEGE
SALISBURY, N. C. 28144

the Iliad, I met Dr. Young in the street, and upon our falling into that subject, the doctor expressed a great deal of surprise at Tickell's having such a translation by him so long. He said, that it was inconceivable to him; and that there must be some mistake in the matter: that he and Tickell were so intimately acquainted at Oxford, that each used to communicate to the other whatever verses they wrote, even to the least things: that Tickell could not have been busied in so long a work there, without his knowing something of the matter; and that he had never heard a single word of it, till on this occasion. This surprise of Dr. Young, together with what Steele has said against Tickell in relation to this affair, make it highly probable that there was some underhand dealing in that business: and indeed Tickell himself, who is a very fair worthy man, has since in a manner as good as owned it to me.————P.[2]

Pope was rather annoyed by the situation that had been created. Addison was no small foe, and his support of Tickell could well have doomed Pope's hope of financial success. Besides, Pope knew that Tickell was an able Classical scholar; and enemies were already publishing taunts about Pope's presumption in attempting to translate a language in which he was not highly trained. Twice Pope made comments to Spence about his worries regarding the translation. The sheer weight of the work and the worry about its success became almost a traumatic experience to him:

What terrible moments does one feel, after one has engaged for a large work!—In the beginning of my translating the Iliad, I wished anybody would hang me, a hundred times.—It sat so heavily on my mind at first, that I often used to dream of it, and do sometimes still. —When I fell into the method of translating thirty or forty verses before I got up, and piddled with the rest of the morning, it went on easy enough; and when I was thoroughly got into the way of it, I did the rest with pleasure.————P.

The Iliad took me up six years; and during that time, and particularly the first part of it, I was often under great pain and apprehension. Though I conquered the thoughts of it in the day, they would frighten me in the night.—I sometimes, still, even dream of being engaged in that translation; and got about half way through it: and being embarrassed and under dread of never completing it.————P.[3]

After much skirmishing and several misleading statements about publication dates, the first four books of Pope's *Iliad* were published on June 6, 1715; and two days later Tickell's translation of Book I appeared. Comparison was inevitable, as Pope had foreseen; and he was subjected to all manner of attack from the Button's group and other enemies. The situation, however, appealed to people's sense of fair play, and in a short time Oxford University and a majority of London readers proclaimed the superiority of Pope's translation to that of Tickell.

The superiority of Pope's version lay in the fact that although Tickell was a much abler Classical scholar, Pope was a poet. This is not to say that Pope was as deficient in reading Greek as his opponents and especially later eighteenth-century critics have implied. Pope openly admitted his deficiencies as a scholar and told Spence that, "In translating both the Iliad and the Odyssey my usual method was, to take advantage of the first heat; and then to correct each book, first by the original text, then by other translations: and lastly to give it a reading for the versification only." [4]

The Preface to the *Iliad* clearly shows that Pope recognized the insuperable difficulties posed by the translation and that he translated as a poet projecting into the idiom of his own day the poetry of another poet from a remote age and language. As an admiring reader of Dryden, Pope knew that Dryden had faced these same problems and had concluded that only three possible ways of translation were open to a translator. The first was "metaphrase," or a word-by-word translation which attempted to transfer literally a poem from one language to another. Being a poet, Pope knew that this was impossible. A second method noted by Dryden was "imitation," or a new and original poem written in the spirit of the original. Pope's "Epistle to Dr. Arbuthnot" is probably the classic example in English of this kind, but an "imitation" is not a translation and would not suffice for the long epic. Dryden's third classification was "paraphrase," a translation which retained those qualities of a poem which are unaffected by connotations of words, such as structure, ideas, narrative, philosophy, characterization, and basic symbols understandable in both languages and times. Retaining these denotative factors, the translator then substituted English idiom for Greek idiom and created new imagery to replace the original which would have little or no meaning because of changes in language or differences in taste, customs, cultures, or civilizations. The result was, in one sense, a new poem; but it was also true to the original in that it made the work meaningful to the new audience. It translated the living experience of the original into experiential terms to which the new reader of a modern age could respond. This method Pope chose for his translation of the *Iliad*.

That Pope was aware that certain qualities of the *Iliad* were translatable and others were not is apparent in his Preface. He begins with praise for Homer's powers of "invention," or genius, which, as the context shows, manifests itself in two major ways. Because of his genius, Homer is, first of all, Nature:

> Nor is it a wonder if he [Homer] has ever been acknowledged the greatest of poets, who most excelled in that which is the very foundation of poetry. It is the invention that, in different degrees, distinguishes all great geniuses: the utmost stretch of human study, learning, and industry, which masters everything besides, can never attain to this. It furnishes Art with all her materials, and without it Judgment itself can at best but 'steal away': for art is only like a prudent steward that lives on managing the riches of Nature.

The second manifestation of Homer's "invention" is found in his effect on the reader:

> It is to the strength of this amazing invention we are to attribute that unequalled fire and rapture which is so forcible in Homer, that no man of a true poetical spirit is master of himself while he reads him. What he writes is of the most animated nature imaginable; every thing moves, every thing lives, and is put in action. If a council be called, or a battle fought, you are not coldly informed of what was said or done as from a third person: the reader is hurried out of himself by the force of the poet's imagination, and turns in one place to a hearer, in another to a spectator.

Throughout these introductory remarks, Pope's comparisons of Homer with other writers (Virgil, Lucan, Statius, Milton, Shakespeare) make it obvious that no translator or poet could hope to reproduce these qualities of Homer.

But Homer's "invention" also works through channels which can be followed in translation:

> Having now spoken of the beauties and defects of the original, it remains to treat of the translation, with the same view to the chief characteristic. As far as that is seen in the main parts of the poem, such as the fable, manners, and sentiments, no translator can prejudice it but

by wilful omissions or contractions. As it also breaks out in every particular image, description, and simile, whoever lessens or too much
softens those, takes off from this chief character. It is the first grand
duty of an interpreter to give his author entire and unmaimed; and for
the rest, the diction and versification only are his proper province, since
these must be his own, but the others he is to take as he finds them.

Pope believes the translator should faithfully follow the "main
parts of the poem," which are translatable qualities; but he must
create for himself the diction and versification if the translation is
to allow Homer to speak to the eighteenth century.

The first of these elements which can be transferred from the
original is the fable, or plot: "Homer opened a new and boundless
walk for his imagination, and created a world for himself in the
invention of fable. That which Aristotle calls 'the soul of poetry'
was first breathed into it by Homer. I shall begin with considering
him in his part, as it is naturally the first; and I speak of it both as
it means the design of a poem, and as it is taken for fiction."

Pope understood Homer's "fable" as having three elements: the
"probable," the "allegorical," and the "marvellous." The "probable" fable is "the recital of such action as, though they did not
happen, yet might, in the common course of nature; or of such as,
though they did, became fables by the additional episodes and
manner of telling them. . . . That of the Iliad is the 'anger of
Achilles,' the most short and single subject that ever was chosen
by a poet." The "allegorical fable" is representation of "elements,
the qualifications of the mind, the virtues and vices, in forms and
persons; and to introduce them into actions agreeable to the nature of the things they shadowed." The "marvellous fable includes
whatever is supernatural, and especially the machines of the
gods."

Since action requires actors, characterization is the second quality of the original poem which the translator must render in a
fairly literal fashion:

Every one [character] has something so singularly his own, that no
painter could have distinguished them more by their features, than the
poet has by their manners. Nothing can be more exact than the distinctions he has observed in the different degrees of virtues and vices.
The single quality of courage is wonderfully diversified in the several

characters of the Iliad. That of Achilles is furious and intractable; that of Diomede forward, yet listening to advice, and subject to command; that of Ajax is heavy and self-confiding. . . . The main characters of Ulysses and Nestor consist in wisdom; and they are distinct in this, that the wisdom of one is artificial and various, of the other natural, open, and regular.

Pope cautions that the third quality, the speeches of the characters, can be translated only partially. Since language is involved, part of it will be the translator's own; but the speeches must reflect the main temperament of the character because characterization is involved with the unity of the structure and action.

The last translatable quality is Homer's "sentiments." A better word might be "sententiae," as Pope's comment indicates: "What were alone sufficient to prove the grandeur and excellence of his sentiments in general, is, that they have so remarkable a parity with those of the Scripture."

All these elements capable of translation reinforce the fable, which presents the "moral" of the Iliad. As Pope saw it, the "moral" was that "Concord, among Governours, is the preservation of States, and Discord the Ruin of them." This moral is presented by the ordered actions of the "probable" fable; by the symbolic meanings of the "allegorical"; and by the "marvellous" element. The marvelous contributes to the epic's moral through identification of Homer's Zeus with characteristics and attitudes drawn from the Old Testament's Jehovah and Milton's God in *Paradise Lost*. This is also one of the many ways in which Pope makes Homer's primitive religion and mythology palatable and meaningful for his more sophisticated audience. The moral of the fable is further strengthened by Pope's conception of Homer's characters. Each character is not only realistic but is also purposely representational of a virtue or vice; a character, then, by being individual and universal at the same time, helps to fulfill the moral. The speeches of the characters carry the "sentiments," which are also functional in that they illustrate the action, help characterize the speaker, and implement the moral.

In placing so much emphasis on the "moral" of the epic, Pope was contributing to the epic tradition as he understood it.[5] To him, the tradition was not even remote, let alone dead. His views of the heroic tradition were somewhat akin to those of T. S. Eliot, whose firm belief in the continuity of tradition is expressed in "Tradition and the Individual Talent" and in "The Function of Criticism." To Pope the heroic tradition was a living thing which gave in the present new life to the past, through such works as Spenser's *Faerie Queene,* Milton's *Paradise Lost,* and Dryden's translation of the *Aeneid.* And the heroic tradition of the past gives sinews and muscle to the present through those poets who carried its impulse forward. He had also expressed this belief in the "Essay on Criticism":

> Be *Homer's* Works your *Study,* and *Delight,*
> Read them by Day, and meditate by Night,
> Thence form your Judgment, thence your Maxims bring,
> And trace the Muses *upward* to their *Spring.* (ll. 124–27)

An important refinement in epic theory made by Renaissance critics and humanists concerned the epic hero. The critics based their prescriptions for the epic hero on their understanding of Aristotle. Because Aristotle had linked epic and tragedy in one respect, namely their actions—tragedy being dramatic and epic being narrative—Italian and French critics felt justified in extending the comparison to the moral nature of the protagonist. The epic hero, they analogized from Aristotelian dicta on tragedy, should display a virtue which illustrates the moral purpose of the epic. The humanists, too, distorted the teaching of Aristotle. In trying to adapt classical literature to educational and didactic ends, they maintained that the classical epics taught a moral lesson. Pope's age thus read the *Iliad* and *Odyssey* as literary epics, as one would read the *Aeneid.* The rather simple but courageous warrior became an aristocratic prince, an example of the good life.

Even if Pope had completely understood Homeric civilization, he could not have made it meaningful to his own time as a poetic experience in any literal way. He had to interpret Homer, not reproduce him historically, for the eighteenth century. And, believing as he did that the heroic tradition was alive, Pope had to base it on eighteenth-century values, while noting differences as well as similarities between Homeric and eighteenth-century civilization. Pope had to accomplish most of this through language and poetic qualities, but some of it had already been achieved through the Renaissance modification of epic theory and the practice of Milton and Dryden.

To acclimate his translation to the eighteenth century, Pope cast it into the heroic couplet, a fact which subjected him in his own time to criticism from his enemies but even more so toward the end of the century when the couplet was disparaged by the Romantics. Wiser than some of his contemporary critics, Pope knew that the very nature of the English language forbade transferring the unrhymed Greek hexameter verse form of Homer based upon quantity into English, which was accentual, not quantitative. This battle had been fought during the Renaissance, and rhyme had been victorious. Even Chapman's translation of the *Iliad* had used rhymed couplets, although it had tried to reproduce the Greek hexameter by using a fourteen-syllable line. The closest approximation to quantity in English would be blank verse, and in Milton's *Paradise Lost* Pope would have had good precedent for translating into that verse form. But he was aware, as his remarks to Spence concerning *Paradise Lost* indicate, that blank verse was better adapted to a subject which was exotic and remote from this physical world. The *Iliad* constantly relates man to his world. Moreover, to use the style of Milton would be to run the almost certain risk of parodying *Paradise Lost*.

Pope was left, then, with the heroic couplet for his translation. This verse form, used properly, possessed the qualities necessary for epic language: elegance, refinement, precision, and, above all, a remoteness from ordinary speech. Pope had mastered the couplet in his experimentation and could use it to create the aura of ceremony and formality necessary to the heroic world. Rhyme, as Pope's translation shows, could be used to bind together a series of couplets into an episode—essential to the rapid action of the *Iliad*—and, at the same time, beneath the action, it could supplement and order the total meaning of the passage by commenting upon the action.

The following lines create the feeling of rapid action which Pope accomplished within the couplet form:

> Now had the Grecians snatch'd a short repast,
> And buckled on their shining arms with haste.
> Troy roused as soon; for on this dreadful day

The fate of fathers, wives, and infants lay.
The gates unfolding pour forth all their train;
Squadrons on squadrons cloud the dusky plain:
Men, steeds, and chariots shake the trembling ground:
The tumult thickens, and the skies resound;
And now with shouts the shocking armies closed,
To lances lances, shields to shields opposed,
Host against host with shadowy legends drew,
The sounding darts in iron tempests flew;
Victors and vanquish'd join promiscuous cries,
Triumphant shouts and dying groans arise;
With streaming blood the slippery fields are dyed,
And slaughter'd heroes swell the dreadful tide.
Long as the morning beams, increasing bright,
O'er heaven's clear azure spread the sacred light,
Commutual death the fate of war confounds,
Each adverse battle gored with equal wounds.
But when the sun the height of heaven ascends,
The sire of gods his golden scales suspends,
With equal hand: in these explored the fate
Of Greece and Troy, and poised the mighty weight:
Press'd with its load, the Grecian balance lies
Low sunk on earth, the Trojan strikes the skies.
Then Jove from Ida's top his horrors spreads;
The clouds burst dreadful o'er the Grecian heads;
Thick lightnings flash; the muttering thunder rolls;
Their strength he withers, and unmans their souls.
Before his wrath the trembling hosts retire;
The gods in terrors, and the skies on fire.   (VIII, 67–98)

This passage does several things simultaneously. For one thing, it involves one in the action being described: the reader feels the confusion of the battle in "To lances lances, shields on shields opposed,/Host against host with shadowy legends drew." Also, the language casts the battle in terms of a storm, which more easily relates the incident to the reader's experience: "pour," "cloud," "tumult," "skies," "tempests," "swell . . . tide." At the same time, the couplet organization of the passage detaches the reader from the action and allows him to look upon the event as part of the total movement of the poem: its language is not the reader's spoken language, and this fact sets the action apart, even though his emotions are at times involved in it. Moreover, the action is seen against the background of eternal nature which must view it as only a passing incident in the eternal series of mornings: "Long as the morning beams, increasing bright,/O'er heaven's clear azure spread the sacred light." And, finally, the episode is a manifestation of the divine intervention in the affairs of man, again in imagery of storm:

> Then Jove from Ida's top his horror spreads;
> The clouds burst dreadful o'er the Grecian heads;
> Thick lightnings flash.

This dual use of language, literal and metaphorical, is constant throughout the translation. It serves the immediate descriptive context, but, in turning it to a description of the mental attitude of the Greeks, it also helps maintain the continuity of the whole poem.

Critics from the time of Coleridge to the present day have accused Pope of inventing "poetic diction" in his translation. Obviously, Pope did not invent such a diction, the development of which can be seen in the work of translators covering the hundred years' span before Pope. That lesser imitators saw fit to use his diction unsparingly can hardly be a fault imputed to Pope. Most of this criticism focuses on Pope's use of the compound epithet, a coupling of an abstract noun and a concrete adjective. The space given to this problem in the Preface makes it quite clear that Pope knew exactly what he was doing:

If we descend from hence to the expression, we see the bright imagination of Homer shining out in the most enlivened forms of it. We acknowledge him the father of poetical diction; the first who taught that language of the gods to men. His expression is like the colouring of some great masters, which discovers itself to be laid on boldly, and executed with rapidity. It is, indeed, the strongest and most glowing imaginable, and touched with the greatest spirit. Aristotle had reason to say, he was the only poet who had found out living words; there are in him more daring figures and metaphors than in any good author whatever. An arrow is impatient to be on the wing, a weapon thirsts to drink the blood of an enemy, and the like; yet his expression is never too big for the sense, but justly great in proportion to it. . . .

To throw his language more out of prose, Homer seems to have affected the compound epithet. This was a sort of composition peculiarly proper to poetry; not only as it heightened the diction, but as it assisted and filled the numbers with greater sound and pomp, and likewise conduced in some measure to thicken the images . . . they are a sort of supernumerary pictures of the persons or things to which they were joined. We see the motion of Hector's plumes in the epithet κορυθαίολος ["crest-shaking"], the landscape of Mount Neritus in that of Εἰνοσίφυλλος ["leaf-quivering"], and so of others; which particular images could not have been insisted upon so long as to express them in a description (though but of a single line) without diverting the reader too much from the principal action or figure. As a metaphor is a short simile, one of these epithets is a short description. . . .

This consideration may further serve to answer for the constant use of the same epithets to his gods and heroes; such as the far-darting Phoebus, the blue-eyed Pallas, and swift-footed Achilles, &c., which some have censured as impertinent, and tediously repeated. Those of the gods depended upon the powers and offices then believed to belong to them; and had contracted a weight and veneration from the rites and solemn devotions in which they were used. . . . As for the epithets of great men . . . they might have this also in common with the gods, not to be mentioned with the solemnity of an epithet, and such as might be acceptable to them by celebrating their families, actions, or qualities. . . .

There are two peculiarities in Homer's diction, which are a sort of marks or moles by which every common eye distinguishes him at first sight . . . I speak of his compound epithets, and of his repetitions. Many of the former cannot be done literally into English without destroying the purity of our language. I believe such should be retained as slide easily of themselves into an English compound, without violence to the ear or to the received rules of composition, as well as those which have received a sanction from the authority of our best poets, and are become familiar through their use of them . . .

Some that cannot be so turned, as to preserve their full image by one or two words, may have justice done them by circumlocution. . . .

The epithets, then, are functional in that they contribute to the epic's elevation of language. More important, however, is the fact that the epithets, repetitions, similes, and speeches contribute to the total meaning of the *Iliad* and comment on Homer's and on Pope's view of man. The epithets, for example, help to convey the basic elements of human experience which remained relatively the same in Homer's simpler days and in Pope's more sophisticated age. Mr. Knight's statement concerning the function of these epithets in Homer is relevant to Pope's use of them in his translation:

And all of these ways of speaking [the generalized descriptive word: compound epithets and repetitions] force us to be conscious of the way in which life repeats itself as it changes, the way in which certain aspects of it are permanent through every kind of action. . . .

The fact that men, like natural events, persist in their fundamental qualities is important for the poem because the two kinds of stability have there a constant relation to one another. This relation is built upon a feeling of recurrent *finiteness* in man and an *exhaustless* recurrence of events in nature, which first of all sets up an antithesis between man and nature. We have a contrast in the poem between the assumption that nature is unlimited in time and the recognition that man's repetition of a quality in the actions of his life is always limited by the sureness of his death.[6]

Pope not only follows his original in using the epithet, but he also uses poetic diction with the advice of Horace lingering in his ear: "Careful and nice, too, in his choice of words, the author of the promised poem must reject one word and welcome another; you will have expressed yourself admirably if a clever setting gives a spice of novelty to a familiar word." [7] Pope thus unites the old (abstract) and the new (concrete). The old presents the typical, the universal, or that which is an infinite recurrence in nature; the new represents a fresh way of seeing the recurrent event, the particular, or that which is finite in the present condition of man. Pope's use of the epithet thus allows him to make the experience of the *Iliad* a part of the eighteenth-century experience, not just a historical reconstruction of Homer. The "new" word can relate the "universal" and interpret it to his contemporary world view and thereby allow the heroic tradition to speak to his own day. In using "poetic diction," Pope was continuing a heroic tradition handed down through a century of translators who adapted the Classics for their own generations.

Pope's translation becomes his own not only through diction and versification, as he maintains in his Preface, but also through the variation of meaning between the original and the translation. It could not be otherwise. Homer, writing in a more primitive age about a folk hero, emphasizes the rule of justice as the rule of the universe; and justice, as well as fate, is embodied in Zeus. Such a concept establishes in the universe order, involving both the natural and the supernatural. All characters and all actions must fit this inexorable order of things, and their attempts to frustrate and eventually to conform to the pattern create the tragic element of Homer's epic. Pope, writing in the Renaissance tradition, emphasizes this concept more than Homer did; and Pope makes it less objective, more moral. The translation asserts the triumph of the will of God, or of divine justice. The change is the result of Pope's identification of pagan Zeus with the Christian God, especially as he is shaped by *Paradise Lost*. Pope's Jove (Zeus, but Pope uses Roman names for the Greek) rebukes Juno, who would try to divine his mind:

> To this the Thunderer: "Seek not thou to find
> The sacred counsels of almighty mind:
> Involved in darkness lies the great decree,
> Nor can the depths of fate be pierced by thee.
> What fits thy knowledge, thou the first shalt know;
> The first of gods above, and men below;
> But thou, nor they, shall search the thoughts that roll
> Deep in the close recesses of my soul."   (I, 704–11)

or Hera, who doubts his intentions to fulfill his promises:

> Then thus the god: "O restless fate of pride,
> That strives to learn what heaven resolves to hide;
> Vain is the search, presumptuous and abhorr'd,
> Anxious to thee, and odious to thy lord.
> Let this suffice: the immutable decree
> No force can shake: what is, that ought to be.
> Goddess, submit; nor dare our will withstand,
> But dread the power of this avenging hand:
> The united strength of all the gods above
> In vain resists the omnipotence of Jove."   (I, 726–35)

Jove, embodying absolute justice and fate, sounds much like Milton's God:

> Boundless and Deep, because I am who fill
> Infinitude, nor vacuous the space.
> Though I uncircumscrib'd myself retire,

And put not forth my goodness, which is free
To act or not, Necessity and Chance
Approach not me, and what I will is Fate.
(*Paradise Lost*, VII, 168–73)

Since divine justice establishes order in the universe, man's participation in that order becomes in Pope's translation a moral act; and Pope explores man's involvement in this moral context through the Chain of Being, a concept still strong in the early eighteenth century although science had been steadily destroying it link by link. To sin against order was to sin against God and his reflection, whether in the natural, social, or civil levels of correspondences. A classic example of this is Pope's implicit use of the "Chain," which enriches and reinforces the encounter between Ulysses and Thersites, who, as a slave, in attacking Agamemnon, the King, is not only attacking the social order of the state but also the civil order. In so presenting the encounter, Pope is underscoring his "moral": "that Concord, among Governours, is the preservation of States, and Discord the ruin of them." Pope begins with a physical description of Thersites, which paints his inner nature as well:

> Thersites only clamour'd in the throng,
> Loquacious, loud, and turbulent of tongue:
> Awed by no shame, by no respect controll'd,
> In scandal busy, in reproaches bold:
> With witty malice studious to defame,
> Scorn all his joy, and laughter all his aim:
> But chief he gloried with licentious style
> To lash the great, and monarchs to revile.
> His figure such as might his soul proclaim;
> One eye was blinking, and one leg was lame:
> His mountain shoulders half his breast o'erspread,
> Thin hairs bestrew'd his long misshapen head.
> Spleen to mankind his envious heart possess'd,
> And much he hated all, but most the best:
> Ulysses or Achilles still his theme;
> But royal scandal his delight supreme,
> Long had he lived the scorn of every Greek,
> Vex'd when he spoke, yet still they heard him speak.
> Sharp was his voice; which in the shrillest tone,
> Thus with injurious taunts attack'd the throne.   (II, 255–75)

After Thersites' slanderous and insolent attack on Agamemnon, Ulysses upbraids him:

> Fierce from his seat at this Ulysses springs,
> In generous vengeance of the king of kings.
> With indignation sparkling in his eyes,
> He views the wretch, and sternly thus replies:
>   'Peace, factious monster, born to vex the state,
> With wrangling talents form'd for foul debate:
> Curb that impetuous tongue, nor rashly vain,
> And singly mad, asperse the sovereign reign.
> Have we not known thee, slave! of all our host,
> The man who acts the least, upbraids the most?
> Think not the Greeks to shameful flight to bring,
> Nor let those lips profane the name of king.
> For our return we trust the heavenly powers;
> Be that their care; to fight like men be ours.   (II, 303–16)

The imagery constantly relates the idea of order to the divine, the social, and the civil order.

In illustrating his concept of divine justice and order by the Chain of Being, Pope is making Homer's world and moral values intelligible to his own century. He is thus enabled to make the *Iliad*, remote in time and place, reflect basic aspects of the way in which men think, feel, and act when responsibility is placed upon them and when they are thrust into the pattern of immutable order and divine justice.

Richard Bentley's reputed comment to Pope concerning the translation, "It's a very pretty poem, but you mustn't call it Homer," has its element of truth. It was impossible to render the *Iliad* into English literally; and, had it been possible, it would have been worthless as poetry. Pope translated as a poet and produced a translation that recreated the experience of the original for his own age. He captured the past for the present, and he informed the present by the past. More than this no translator could do, and the consensus of critical opinion agrees that Pope's translation of the *Iliad* still remains the most exciting, vivid, and, in most respects, the best yet done.

With success assured by the publication in 1715 of the first volume of the *Iliad* containing Books I–IV, Pope continued his translation. He issued Volume II in 1716; Volume III, 1717: Volume IV, 1718; and the final two volumes in 1720. The subscription paid Pope so handsomely that his financial future was secure. Pope is often with good cause referred to as the shrewdest businessman among English poets. Doubtless the financial success of the *Iliad* led him later to continue translating Homer. The first three volumes of the *Odyssey* were published in 1725, and volumes IV–V in 1726. This time, however, he employed Elijah Fenton and William Broome to do much of the laborious translation, which he then revised into its final form. Pope's letters to Broome urge secrecy in the matter. Probably the two translators knew that Pope's reputation would assure a greater sale than their own, so they agreed that the work would come out under his name alone. The facts, however, became known; and Pope, unable to admit or deny the assistance, was at the mercy of his enemies. When the *Odyssey*, despite the adverse publicity, was successful, Pope's financial position became even more secure.

II   *"An Elegy to the Memory of an Unfortunate Lady";*
         "Eloisa to Abelard"

After the continued success of the *Iliad* with the publication of the second volume in 1717, Pope felt it was time to issue a collected volume of his *Works*. Published by Lintot in June, 1717, the *Works* contained several minor poems hitherto unpublished and two more substantial pieces which were to prove lasting favorites: "Verses to the Memory of an Unfortunate Lady" and "Eloisa to Abelard." The two poems are often referred to as Pope's attempts to write in the new style of pre-Romanticism, then coming into vogue. This claim does not have much substance, however, since the poems are based on Classical forms and tradition. Both are indebted to Ovid's *Elegies* and *Epistles,* and in 1736 Pope changed the title of the first poem to "An Elegy to the Memory of an Unfortunate Lady." The "Elegy" seems to belong more properly to the earlier experimental period of Pope's work.

A strange mixture of Elizabethan diction, metaphysical wit, theatrical devices from the contemporary "she-tragedies" of his friend Nicholas Rowe (dagger, ghost, exaggerated gloom), pathos, slight irony, sententiousness, the "Elegy" has a mysterious, personal, almost autobiographical conclusion. The concluding hint of Pope's involvement in a love affair is probably the factor which made the poem a success. At its publication his old friend John Caryll wrote Pope asking who the "unfortunate" lady was. Since that day, critics have been trying to identify her, despite the fact that Pope carefully refused to divulge her name. Very likely, the poet knew that a little mystery would never diminish the success of a love story.

"Eloisa to Abelard," an Ovidian heroic epistle after the manner of Drayton's *England's Heroicall Epistles,* is a better controlled poem in which the contrasting elements are integrated and sustained throughout. In the "Elegy" the diction, and often the tone, varies according to whatever element is at the moment dominant; but in "Eloisa to Abelard" the contrast of emotion, scene, and tone is deliberate, ordered, and at all times contributes to one's understanding of Eloisa's predicament, this conflict being the theme of the poem. Perhaps the poem is more successful than its companion piece because Pope is telling a public story, not a personal or feigned one. He based his poem mainly on Eloisa's first letter to Abelard, taken from a series of letters translated into English in 1713 by John Hughes. This first letter surveys Eloisa's past relationship with Abelard in chronological order. Pope follows this organization but he brings the time sequence up to the present so that Eloisa may realize her situation—and then he extends it into the future as she resolves her conflict by choosing death over obedience to her vows.

The structure of the poem is based on contrast. Eloisa remembers a past scene with Abelard with its attendant emotion and tone, and she contrasts it with her present predicament with its dominant emotion and tone. In whatever terms the contrast may be stated in any given scene, Pope's imagery shows that it is a manifestation of Eloisa's psychological state: her prayers to God for help are, beneath the surface, lovers' vows; love of God has become for her an erotic experience. Even death, the only solution to her conflict, is revealed by the imagery to be erotic satisfaction.

With the exception of the few new poems in the *Works* of 1717, Pope found little time for creative work in the period from 1715 to 1725. When his friend John Caryll wrote him in 1722 complaining of this state of affairs, Pope replied as follows: "I must again sincerely protest to you, that I have wholly given over scribbling, at least anything of my own, but am become, by due gradation of dulness, from a poet a translator, and from a translator, a mere editor. Were I really capable at this time of producing anything, I should be incapable of concealing it from you, who have been so many years one of my best critics, as well as one of my best friends." [8] After the translation of the *Iliad* he busied himself in the early 1720's with editing the works of three other writers: Thomas Parnell; John Sheffield, Duke of Buckingham; and Shakespeare.

III *Editions of Parnell and Sheffield*

The Reverend Thomas Parnell (1679–1718) was one of Pope's oldest friends, their friendship dating back to the days of the Pope-Wycherley association. An Irishman who had settled in England, Parnell had written *Guardian* essays at the time of Pope's intimacy with Addison and Steele; and he had on several occasions defended Pope in print against Dennis' fulminations. When Parnell died in 1718, he left to Pope, his literary executor, the manuscripts that Pope published as *Poems on Several Occasions* (1721). As a letter written in 1720 to Charles Jervas, the painter, reveals, Pope published only those poems which he felt would heighten Parnell's reputation:

This [a desire to see Jervas] awakens the memory of some of those who have made a part in all these. Poor *Parnelle, Garth, Rowe!* You justly reprove me for not speaking of the Death of the last: *Parnelle* was too much in my mind, to whose Memory I am erecting the best Monument I can. What he gave me to publish, was but a small part of what he left behind him, but it was the best, and I will not make it worse by enlarging it. I'd fain know if he be buried at *Chester,* or *Dublin;* and what care has been, or is to be taken for his Monument, &c. [9]

Pope's edition of John Sheffield's works, however, was not to prove so innocuous as that of Parnell's. Pope's friendship with Sheffield dated as far back as 1706 at least; at that time Pope had sought his advice on the "Pastorals." He praised Sheffield's verse in the "Essay on Criticism" (ll. 719–824), and Sheffield repaid the compliment with verses of high praise for Pope that were prefixed to the 1717 *Works.* Later Pope wrote two choruses for Sheffield's tragedy *Brutus;* and, after Sheffield's death, Pope announced his intention of editing his papers in a letter to John Caryll in 1722: "Tho' I can give you no good account of myself as to any things of my own, yet I am very busy in doing justice to a far greater poet [Shakespeare], of whose works I am giving a new edition. Besides this, I have the care of overlooking the Duke of Buckingham's papers, and correcting the press. That will be a very beautiful book, and has many things in it you will be particularly glad to see in relation to some former reigns." [10]

Although Pope undoubtedly was motivated by loyalty to an old friend, this decision was unfortunate. Sheffield had had Jacobite tendencies, and the fact that Pope was Roman Catholic rendered him politically suspect. Moreover, Pope's friend Bishop Atterbury was committed to the Tower of London in August, 1722, on charges of treason—charges based mainly on his correspondence with the Pretender and his suspected participation in a plot to restore the Stuarts to the throne. Pope realized the seriousness of the situation and tried to drop the editing of Sheffield's papers; but Sheffield's widow urged him to continue. On January 24, 1723 the two volumes appeared, only to be confiscated three days later by the government. By March, however, the prohibition against Sheffield's *Works* was lifted and copies were again on sale. Meanwhile, Pope had been called as a witness in Atterbury's trial before the House of Lords, and this incident subjected him once again to violent Whig and anti-Catholic attacks in the press.

IV *Edition of Shakespeare*

During all this activity Pope had been at work on an edition of Shakespeare's plays. It cannot be determined when or precisely why he undertook the project. On October 21, 1721 he inserted an advertisement in the *Evening Post* asking help from anyone having information concerning Shakespeare's plays and texts, and so it is likely that he began the work about this time. Inasmuch as the subscription for the edition was in the name of Jacob Tonson, the publisher, Pope probably agreed to do the work for a share of the profits. Professor George Sherburn reports that Tonson paid Pope £217 12s. for the edition,[11] and Pope later complained in print that the subscription was for Tonson, not for him.

But Pope's interest in editing Shakespeare may not have been altogether monetary. He had always admired Shakespeare as a poet, but the irregularity of his plays caused Pope to describe them in the Preface as "an ancient majestick piece of *Gothick* Architecture having dark, odd, and uncouth passages." This fault, however, Pope could excuse because Shakespeare, an actor, catered to the low tastes of his audience for success; also, since Shakespeare had lived in an ignorant time, he was not to be judged by Aristotle's rules. Beyond these cavils, "The Poetry of *Shakespear* was Inspiration indeed: he is not so much an Imitator, as an Instrument of Nature; and 'tis not so just to say that he speaks from her, as that she speaks thro' him."

Also, although one does not usually think of Pope in relation to the drama, he had always a strong interest in it; this interest dates back perhaps to his earliest schooldays at Twyford when he composed a tragedy from speeches in Ogilvy's translation of the *Iliad*. His first literary friends were of the theater: Wycherley, Congreve, Thomas Southerne, and the actor Thomas Betterton. Throughout his busy career he found time to advise and often to touch up the plays of Addison, Gay, Sheffield, John Hughes, Elijah Fenton, Nicholas Rowe, David Lewis, Aaron Hill, James Thomson, and David Mallet. For the plays of several of these friends, he wrote prologues and epilogues. In at least one instance Pope tried his own hand at drama. He collaborated with Arbuthnot and Gay in a Scriblerian farce, *Three Hours after Marriage*, produced at Drury Lane Theatre on January 17, 1717. It is, therefore, conceivable that Pope's interest in the theater and his genuine desire to raise its quality—a desire evinced in several of his satires—were determining factors in his acceptance of Tonson's offer to edit Shakespeare.

The audiences of Pope's time did not see Shakespeare's plays as they had been written. The more "regular" taste of the period had caused Shakespeare's *Lear* to be replaced by Nahum Tate's version; Davenant's adaptation of *Macbeth* and *The Tempest* were preferred to Shakespeare's; Dryden's *All for Love* had superseded *Antony and Cleopatra;* and Colley Cibber's *Richard III* had replaced the original. Moreover, to give the reading public the true text of Shakespeare would be a service to poetry.

Unfortunately, Pope did not restore Shakespeare's original text —despite his bold claim in the Preface that he had "discharged the dull duty of an Editor, to my best judgment . . . with an abhorrence of all innovation, and without any indulgence to my private sense or conjecture." Perhaps he failed because, as is evident from his letters to Tonson, Fenton, and Broome, he hired assistants and used the help of his friends to do the drudgery of the actual textual work and footnoting. And a letter to Tonson indicates Pope's rather social but somewhat unscientific method of collating texts: "I'm resolv'd to pass the next whole week in London, purposely to get together Parties of my acquaintance ev'ry night, to collate the several Editions of Shakespear's single Plays, 5 of which I have ingaged to this design. You shall then hear of me." [12]

Pope seems to have done little more than follow the text printed by Nicholas Rowe, his friend and the first editor of Shakespeare (1709). Rowe's text had been based on the fourth folio, and Pope emended the 1709 text, utilizing no discernible principles of textual emendation (except for an occasional change made on the evidence of a quarto), relying solely on his poetic taste and finely attuned ear. As a matter of fact, Pope's metrical emendations have withstood fairly well the rigorous scrutiny of subsequent editors. Little else of his work, however, has survived modern textual scholarship.

One fact should be pointed out in Pope's defense. The text he produced, as is evident in his footnotes and system of asterisks and commas to point out the "shining passages," was to raise Shakespeare in the estimation of the early eighteenth-century reader. His was not a text for scholars; nor was it an attempt to provide the theater with a true text for production. Almost all of the low scenes, extravagances, and grotesqueries, which Pope relegated to the smaller type at the bottom of the page, would have been offensive to readers of his day. Some of these scenes Pope refused to believe Shakespeare wrote. Professor John Butt has pointed out that Pope's taste in Shakespeare focused on descriptive passages, sententiae, and set speeches by the characters.[18] These qualities would also have been appreciated by Pope's contemporaries.

When the six volumes appeared in March, 1725, the edition was severely criticized for its high price, but the criticism soon moved to caustic comment about textual deficiencies. The controversy reached its climax in March, 1726, when Lewis Theobald published *Shakespeare Restored: or a Specimen of the Many Errors, as well Committed, as Unamended, by Mr. Pope In his Late Edition of this Poet.* Theobald was a scholar, well-read in Elizabethan literature; and, while his corrections of Pope have suffered considerable further correction by succeeding textual scholars, he proved beyond any doubt the insufficiencies of Pope as an editor. Evidently Pope realized that his reputation as an editor was ruined, for he did no more editing from them on. In time Theobald reappeared in Pope's life; and, when he did, it was as king of the dunces in the first version of the "Dunciad."

CHAPTER 3

The Moralized Song

IN THE poetic apologia for his life and work, the "Epistle to Dr. Arbuthnot," Pope comments:

> That not in Fancy's Maze he wander'd long,
> But stoop'd to Truth, and moraliz'd his song:
> That not for Fame, but Virtue's better end,
> He stood the furious Foe, the timid Friend,
> The damning Critic, half-approving Wit,
> The Coxcomb hit, or fearing to be hit;
> Laughed at the loss of Friends he never had,
> The dull, the proud, the wicked, and the mad;
> The distant Threats of Vengeance on his head,
> The Blow unfelt, the Tear he never shed;
> The Tale reviv'd, the Lye so oft o'erthrown;
> Th' imputed Trash, and Dulness not his own;
> The Morals blacken'd when the Writings scape;
> The libel'd Person, and the pictur'd Shape;
> Abuse on all he lov'd, or lov'd him, spread,
> A friend in Exile, or a Father, dead;
> The Whisper that to Greatness still too near,
> Perhaps, yet vibrates on his SOVEREIGN's Ear—
> Welcome for thee, fair Virtue! all the past:
> For thee, fair Virtue! welcome ev'n the *last!*   (ll. 340–59)

The question has often been raised and as often answered as to why Pope left behind the realm of the highly imaginative in order to devote the remainder of his life to satire. The answer most often heard is that, having been stung for ten years by repeated libels and unjustified attacks, he finally began counterattacking. Such an answer is dictated largely by the nineteenth-century prejudiced view of Pope as the little "wasp of Twickenham" who was occupied with stinging and annoying the critics whom he had maliciously aroused in the first place.

The lines quoted above convey the impression that there is some small truth in the accusation. And there can be no doubt that the "Dunciad Variorum" of 1729, which replaced the initials in the 1728 edition with the actual names of enemies, forced Pope's adversaries into a concerted attempt to make it appear a document of personal revenge. Professor Rogers, a most able student of Pope, concludes that "much of his later poetry reflects his desire to correct the portrait of his moral character to which the dunces had given currency. . . . thus Pope was stimulated to strenuous efforts to create a lasting monument to his genius. Such stimulation largely made possible the *Essay on Man,* the *Ethic Epistles,* and the *Imitations of Horace.* We cannot therefore regret Pope's attempt to pay off his enemies." [1] While such a conclusion as Professor Rogers draws contains an element of truth, to weight such an element so heavily somewhat distorts the whole picture.

It is highly probable that the reawakening of Pope's dormant creative activity was in part the result of Swift's two prolonged visits during the 1720's to Twickenham. The two men reviewed their work and talked over the old days, and one result of their reunion was the publication of three volumes of the Pope-Swift *Miscellanies.* Swift's own creative impulse was satiric and the writing which resulted from it didactic. Pope's work, even while he had wandered in "Fancy's Maze," had cast an ironic shadow; and it was no great transformation to change the shadow into the more substantial body of satire.

Also, the Pope-Swift conversations must have revived memories of the Scriblerus days when the Tories had governed under Queen Anne and writers had been honored. Since those golden days, ten years of Whig rule had produced political corruption and bribery, social and moral disintegration, and eclipse for writers as the star of the scientists and the mathematicians rose. The whole moral fabric of society and the sense of order on which it was erected seemed threatened by the growing emphasis on the individual under Whig rule. Certainly Pope's own painful experiences with hostile critics would have sharpened his awareness of the chang-

ing patterns of life: his proposal to translate Homer had revealed
the weakness of a great man—Addison; the attempt to give his
age the *Iliad* had subjected him to abuse of the most personal
sort; his refusal to choose political sides had brought unwarranted
criticism by the Buttonian Whigs; his desire to restore Shakespeare's text to readers had again unleashed personal attack; and
his loyalty to an old but dead friend, John Sheffield, Duke
of Buckingham, had caused a punitive government to call him
before a court to question his loyalty. Undoubtedly to Pope, the
more stable, ordered way of life was yielding to a new one in
which all values were chaotic and confused. Pope's decision to
"moralize his song" must have resulted, therefore, more from his
realization of these evils than from any personal desire to retaliate
against his attackers. He had remained silent under their abuse
for a dozen years, and they could now say nothing more about
him than they had in the past.

Pope's satire is the greatest in poetic form which the English
language has produced. Great satire cannot spring only from personal animosity or from irritation. It must have at its very center a
moral idealism to motivate its indignation. Also, to achieve its
moral purpose, satire indirectly presents an ideal nature under
ideal conditions by representing actual nature under intensely
realistic or even exaggerated conditions. Pope's satire grew more
and more realistic in its use of names, incidents, and actual conditions in eighteenty-century England. It is not a far reach from the
implicit irony of, for example, "The Rape of the Lock"—discrepancy between appearance and reality—to the greater discrepancy in satire between the ideal and the exaggerated reality. Both
literary techniques—irony and satire—are metaphoric, differing
largely in degree rather than in kind. As the vision of the ideal
recedes more deeply into the past, the more intense is the intru-
sion of the actual, present reality; and the more heightened becomes the moral indignation at this state of affairs.

A state of mind somewhat akin to such indignation must have
rekindled Pope's creative powers at the close of the 1720's. From
Spence's conversations with him, we learn that Pope envisioned a
series of "Ethic Epistles" which would embody a system of ethics.
Spence dates the first mention of this intent in 1730:

"The first epistle is to be to the whole work, what a scale is to a book of maps; and in this, I reckon, lies my greatest difficulty: not only in settling and ranging the parts of it aright, but in making them agreeable enough to be read with pleasure." This was said in May, 1730, of what he then used to call his Moral Epistles, and what he afterwards called his Essay on Man. He at that time intended to have included in one epistle what he afterwards addressed to Lord Bolingbroke in four.[2]

We learn, however, from a letter of Pope to Swift on November 28, 1729, that he must have had the ethical concept in mind at least by that date since he mentions his "System of Ethics in the Horatian way."

Pope's original plans, however, had undergone considerable modification by 1734, as Spence's reference indicates:

"I have drawn in the plan for my Ethic Epistles much narrower than it was at first."—He mentioned several of the particulars, in which he had lessened it; but as this was in the year 1734, the most exact account of his plan (as it stood then) will best appear from a leaf which he annexed to about a dozen copies of the poem, printed in that year, and sent as presents to some of his most particular friends. Most of these were afterwards called in again; but that which was sent to Mr. Bethel was not. It ran as follows:

INDEX TO THE ETHIC EPISTLES

Book I.   Of the Nature and State of Man.

    Epistle 1.—With respect to the Universe.
            2.—As an Individual.
            3.—With respect to Society.
            4.—With respect to Happiness.
Book II.   Of the Use of Things.
           Of the Limits of Human Reason.
           Of the Use of Learning.
           Of the Use of Wit.
           Of the Knowledge and Characters of Men.
           Of the Particular Characters of Women.
           Of the Principles and Use of Civil and Ecclesiastical Polity.
           Of the Use of Education.
           A View of the Equality of Happiness in the Several Conditions of Men.
           Of the Use of Riches.[3]

Probably Pope had decided by 1734 to drop the plan to unite his ethical poems into a system. A letter of December 19, 1734, to Swift says as much:

I am almost at the end of my Morals, as I've been, long ago, of my Wit; my system is a short one, and my circle narrow. Imagination has no limits, and that is a sphere in which you may move on to eternity; but where one is confirmed to Truth (or to speak more like a human creature, to the appearances of Truth) we soon find the shortness of our Tether. Indeed by the help of a metaphysical chain of ideas, one may extend the circulation, go round and round for ever, without making any progress beyond the point to which Providence has pinn'd us: But this does not satisfy me, who would rather say a little to no purpose, than a great deal.[4]

Of the two Books of the "system" as proposed in 1734, Pope finished better than half. The "Essay on Man" constitutes the first book; of the nine titles under Book II—"Of the Use of Things"—he completed four epistles (the "Moral Essays"); and some of the "Horatian Imitations" dwell to some degree on the subjects listed.

I *"An Essay on Man"*

It is obvious that Pope considered the "Essay on Man" the keystone of the whole edifice of the proposed system. His statements to Spence show this, as does the fact that he tried to protect the poem at publication. The "Essay on Man" was probably written by 1731; but, instead of publishing it, Pope offered the public one of the "ethic epistles," the "Epistle to Burlington" on December 14, 1731, under its first title "Of Taste." His enemies quickly sprang to the attack by identifying the satiric portrait of "Timon" with the Duke of Chandos, a friend of Burlington and of Dr. Arbuthnot and a generous subscriber to Pope's *Iliad*. Pope, alarmed at the outcry against him, feared that the reception of the "Essay on Man" would be similarly prejudiced. To safeguard the "Essay," he published, acknowledging his authorship, two more of the "ethic epistles"—"Epistle to Bathurst: Of the Use of Riches" ("Moral Essay IV") on January 15, 1733; and "Epistle to Cobham: Of the Characters of Men" ("Moral Essay I") on January 16, 1733. He followed these two epistles with an anonymous publication of "The Impertinent, Or a Visit to the Court. A Satyr. By

An Eminent Hand" (Donne's "Fourth Satire") and with the first three epistles of the "Essay on Man": the first on February 20, 1733; the second, March 29; and the third, May 8. On January 24, 1734, Pope published Epistle IV, which completed the "Essay on Man." The scheme succeeded, for the poem was highly praised on all sides. The next year, when the poem was republished in Volume II of the *Works,* Pope acknowledged authorship.

The stated proposition of the "Essay on Man"—"But vindicate the ways of God to Man"—immediately suggests a similarity to *Paradise Lost,* wherein Milton proposes to "assert Eternal Providence,/And justifie the wayes of God to men" (I, 25–26). But the poems are different, for during the sixty-seven years which separated the births of the two poems, the intellectual climate had been changing. The problems of both remain somewhat the same, but the attempts to solve them differ. Milton's poem offers an explanation of man's relation to God and of the problem of evil in traditional theological terms—the Fall of Man and the entrance of sin into the world, and the advent of Christ who offered the possibility of salvation through grace. Pope's solution is as traditional and conservative as that of Milton, but it is philosophical and ethical where Milton's had been Christian and theological.

Professor Maynard Mack's description of the Augustan poet's treatment of such subject matter admirably sums up the change from Milton's time: "The subject of Augustan literature is predominantly man in his public aspects—general human nature—the permanent relations of human beings in society . . . When it turns to subjects like religion, or any of the great sources of human emotion, it tends to treat them in their public aspects: philosophical, social, moral; it does not record, like Donne's or Herbert's religious poems, the devotional act itself; or like much romantic poetry, the contours of individual feeling." [5]

Although the "Essay on Man" is not an exposition of Christian doctrine it is not anti-Christian. A cursory reading of any section of it quickly reveals through imagery from Christianity, the Scriptures, and the Church Fathers that Christian ideas are always just beneath the surface of the poem. But the poem treats its theme from philosophical, ethical, social, and psychological points of view without advocating explicit Christian dogmas or doctrines.

Its view of man is basically that of Milton's poem: man is unregenerate, and he must find his salvation.

Pope's solution is worked out in terms of man's discovering, accepting, and enjoying his "middle state" in the divine scheme of things. The middle state, a reconciliation of extremes, is Pope's definition of virtue. Such a middle state is in accord with nature which, operating through the Chain of Being, had placed man at the crossroads of creation; he joined and embodied within himself the upper spiritual and the lower material halves of creation. By partaking of both natures—spiritual and material—man is the microcosm reflecting the divine order of the macrocosm. Since the order which placed man in this middle state is divine, man's questioning of his place is audacious:

> Of Systems possible, if 'tis confest
> That Wisdom infinite must form the best,
> Where all must full or not coherent be,
> And all that rises, rise in due degree;
> Then, in the scale of reas'ning life, 'tis plain
> There must be, somewhere, such a rank as Man;
> And all the question (wrangle e'er so long)
> Is only this, if God has plac'd him wrong? (I, 43–50)

This philosophical question is, then, the focal point about which Epistle I (Of the Nature and State of Man, with Respect to the Universe) revolves.

The divine order of the universe is one "Where all must full or not coherent be,/And all that rises, rise in due degree." There is, therefore, great variety in creation; and man's envy of some of the superior qualities of this variety causes him to question his own place and characteristics. The very questioning of the divine order implies that it is faulty, less perfect than it must be in a divine system ordained by "Wisdom infinite." Evil, then, exists in this "best of Systems possible." But evil cannot be laid to the charge of divine Providence. Even evil must have meaning in the scheme of things, or "Wisdom infinite" is more finite than man's; faith in the system is impossible; and justice cannot exist within its framework.

The universe, then, is meaningful, despite the evil which exists in it. Pope readily admits the existence of evil; and, even though he advances arguments against it, he accepts the problem of evil as insoluble. Pope presents the three kinds of evil which had been recognized for centuries by traditional philosophers and by church fathers. The first is an evil caused by man's misunderstanding of the Chain of Being. The nature of God had caused the nature of the created universe: plenitude and order. There must be an infinite variety among created things so that God's nature is fully realized, and the variety must be hierarchical. This order among created things is part of the meaning of the universe, and to rebel against it is to revolt against Providence itself:

> In Pride, in reas'ning Pride, our error lies;
> All quit their sphere, and rush into the skies.
> Pride still is aiming at the blest abodes,
> Men would be Angels, Angels would be Gods.
> Aspiring to be Gods, if Angels fell,
> Aspiring to be Angels, Men rebel;
> And who but wishes to invert the laws
> Of ORDER, sins against th'Eternal Cause.   (I, 123–30)

It is this hierarchy which makes all parts of creation one; it reconciles extremes into a oneness by means of the *discordia concors* (seen earlier in "Windsor Forest")—the "friendly discord," in which each widely opposing aspect of creation contributes its particular segment to the whole, thus establishing the divine order and the equilibrium which constitute the universe. Man, unable to see this whole and as a consequence seeing only his own segment and feeling that he is in opposition to other segments, rebels against this divine order because of his pride. He wants to be more spiritual, less physical; or he wants physical powers which are the prime characteristic of a lower segment in the scale. This rebellion occasioned by pride is the central theme of the first epistle of "An Essay on Man." The "fall" of man for Pope is man's breaking of nature's union. The other evils discussed in Epistle I are related to this rebellion caused by man's pride which blinds him to the universal harmony of the creation.

The second type of evil is natural, a physical catastrophe such as an earthquake or a flood:

> But errs not Nature from this gracious end,
> From burning suns when livid deaths descend,
> When earthquakes swallow, or when tempests sweep
> Towns to one grave, whole nations to the deep?
> 'No ('tis reply'd) the first Almighty Cause
> 'Acts not by partial, but by gen'ral laws;
> 'Th' exceptions few; some change since all began,
> 'And what created perfect?'—Why then Man?   (I, 141–48)

The "gen'ral Laws" by which "the first Almighty Cause/Acts" do not exist solely for man's sake; they exist for the whole of nature. Therefore, in fulfilling their duty to the whole, they sometimes work to the disadvantage of the part—man. Rainfall is essential to all life; God, therefore, cannot be blamed for a flood (an evil) because He created rain for the good of the whole. Man's complaint against Providence because of such physical evils is again the result of his pride; he sees only what is best for his own limited sphere, not for the whole.

The third evil is moral:

> If plagues or earthquakes break not Heav'n's design,
> Why then a Borgia, or a Cataline?
> Who knows but He, whose hand the light'ning forms,
> Who heaves old Ocean, and who wings the storms,
> Pours fierce Ambition in a Caesar's mind,
> Or turns young Ammon loose to scourge mankind?
> From pride, from pride, our very reas'ning springs;
> Account for moral as for nat'ral things:
> Why charge we heav'n in those, in these acquit?
> In both, to reason right is to submit.   (I, 156–64)

As a little world reflecting within himself the variety and strife of the whole world, man is composed of psychic elements which must be harmonized. He was created with both reason and emotion as parts of his psychic nature, and the emotional part is essential in motivating his conduct. But the emotions must be governed by reason. If they are not, a monstrous, immoral human being—a Borgia or a Cataline—results. Again, the nature of man, created that he may function properly, cannot be blamed if man disregards reason and allows his emotions to pervert his true nature.

Man's pride, then, is responsible for each of these three evils. His violation of the divine order is his fall, and his regeneration lies in his accepting his position in the scheme of things. The theme might be stated in the Socratic truism, "Know thyself." Man, knowing himself aright, participates in the *discordia concors,* the reconciliation of warring opposites, and contributes to "Universal Harmony":

> Cease then, nor ORDER Imperfection name:
> Our proper bliss depends on what we blame.
> Know thy own point: This kind, this due degree
> Of blindness, weakness, Heav'n bestows on thee.
> Submit—
> . . . .
> All Nature is but Art, unknown to thee;
> All Chance, Direction, which thou canst not see;
> All Discord, Harmony, not understood;
> All partial Evil, universal Good:
> And, spite of Pride, in erring Reason's spite,
> One truth is clear, "Whatever is, is Right."
> (I, 281–85, 289–94)

"Whatever is, is right," but man must have faith in the whole in order to live at peace in his own sphere.

Epistle II (Of the Nature and State of Man with Respect to Himself, as an Individual) grows out of Epistle I in that it develops a psychology of man's total nature so that he may truly know himself and move toward regeneration:

> Know then thyself, presume not God to scan;
> The proper study of Mankind is Man.
> Plac'd on this isthmus of a middle state,
> A being darkly wise, and rudely great:
> With too much knowledge for the Sceptic side,
> With too much weakness for the Stoic pride,
> He hangs between; in doubt to act, or rest,
> In doubt to deem himself a God, or Beast;
> In doubt his Mind or Body to prefer,
> Born but to die, and reas'ning but to err;
> Alike in ignorance, his reason such,
> Whether he thinks too little, or too much:

> Chaos of Thought and Passion, all confus'd;
> Still by himself abus'd, or disabus'd;
> Created half to rise, and half to fall;
> Great lord of all things, yet a prey to all;
> Sole judge of Truth, in endless Error hurl'd:
> The glory, jest, and riddle of the world!   (II, 1–18)

Because man is "Plac'd on this isthmus of a middle state," he is
torn with an inner strife between his two natures: one pulls him
upward toward the spiritual and angelic level; the other, downward toward the animal. Sometimes man, misled by pride, thinks
himself all intellect; and, embracing Platonic philosophy or Eastern mysticism, he denies the other part of his nature:

> Go, soar with Plato to th' empyreal sphere,
> To the first good, first perfect, and first fair;
> Or tread the mazy round his follow'rs trod,
> And quitting sense call imitating God;
> As eastern priests in giddy circles run,
> And turn their heads to imitate the Sun.   (II, 23–28)

But this view, Pope believes, denies the reality and complexity of
human nature and character:

> Two Principles in human nature reign;
> Self-love, to urge, and Reason, to restrain;
> Nor this a good, nor that a bad, we call,
> Each works its end, to move or govern all:
> And to their proper operation still,
> Ascribe all Good; to their improper, Ill.   (II, 53–58)

Man's actions—the result of the motivating emotions—must be
guided by reason, which turns the selfishly motivated action into a
benevolent one. Thus an action which in its genesis could be con-
strued as evil (directed toward the self) can be re-directed into a
good (toward the best interests of mankind):

> Th' Eternal Art educing good from ill,
> Grafts on this passion our best principle:
> 'Tis thus the Mercury of Man is fix'd,

> Strong grows the Virtue with his nature mix'd;
> The dross cements what else were too refin'd,
> And in one interest body acts with mind.   (II, 175–80)

Since man is created with these two principles within himself, he is not the free moral agent Milton's man was. He therefore does not create the course his life will follow; but within the determined capacity for possible action he can act for either good or evil. Thus man's actions create an ethical context within which he moves and has his being.

The differences in the personalities of men are accounted for by the "ruling Passion," a single innate emotion which dominates all other appetitive instincts and thus makes possible a stable, recognizable character in a man. It develops in conformity with man's physical and intellectual life:

> As Man, perhaps, the moment of his breath,
> Receives the lurking principle of death;
> The young disease, that must subdue at length,
> Grows with his growth, and strengthens with his strength:
> So, cast and mingled with his very frame,
> The Mind's disease, its ruling Passion came;
> Each vital humour which should feed the whole,
> Soon flows to this, in body and in soul.
> Whatever warms the heart, or fills the head,
> As the mind opens, and its functions spread,
> Imagination plies her dang'rous art,
> And pours it all upon the peccant part.
>   Nature its mother, Habit is its nurse;
> Wit, Spirit, Faculties, but make it worse;
> Reason itself but gives it edge and pow'r;
> As Heav'n's blest beam turns vinegar more sowr.   (II, 133–48)

Pope derived the concept of the ruling passion from the medieval and Renaissance doctrine of "humors." As early as Chaucer, the humoral doctrine of personality and character had appeared in English literature. Chaucer's Wife of Bath, for example, had been born under the sign of Mars and Venus; and the dominating components of her personality were therefore choler and blood—the "humors" corresponding to the planets which influenced her birth. Her personality in turn helped mould her moral character. All Renaissance dramatists founded their characterizations on the

"humor" concept. Ben Jonson in particular gave a moral twist to
the older psychology and presented a vice (or virtue) as the dominant character trait, to which all other character traits were sub-
servient. The "humor" doctrine also figures prominently in the extremely popular seventeenth-century character sketches of Overbury, Hall, and Earle.

In Pope, as in Ben Jonson's comedies, this doctrine is used
satirically to present a distortion of human character with a moral
end in view. Pope does not use the concept satirically in Epistle II
of the "Essay on Man." Rather, he considers the ruling passion as
that principle which makes possible the *discordia concors* in the
individual. It reconciles the discordant, selfish elements in man's
nature with his reason and thus establishes order and stability in
the changeable human being; it makes man a reflection of the
divine order in the universe. From this state of harmony within
man proceeds virtue, that balance between reason and emotions
which fulfills not only the individual's needs but also those of the
whole social organism:

> Virtuous and vicious ev'ry Man must be,
> Few in th'extreme, but all in the degree;
> The rogue and fool by fits is fair and wise,
> And ev'n the best, by fits, what they despise.
> 'Tis but by parts we follow good or ill,
> For, Vice or Virtue, Self directs it still;
> Each individual seeks a sev'ral goal;
> But HEAV'N's great view is One, and that the Whole:
>
> . . . .
>
> That Virtue's ends from Vanity can raise,
> Which seeks no int'rest, no reward but praise;
> And build on wants, and on defects of mind,
> The joy, the peace, the glory of Mankind.
> Heav'n forming each on other to depend,
> A master, or a servant, or a friend,
> Bids each on other for assistance call,
> 'Till one man's weakness grows the strength of all.
> Wants, frailties, passions, closer still ally
> The common int'rest, or endear the tie:
> To these we owe true friendship, love sincere,
> Each home-felt joy that life inherits here:
> (II, 231–38, 245–56)

The ruling passion allied with reason allows that virtue nearest our vice to become dominant; lust becomes love, or self-love becomes love of others. In this manner, the ruling passion makes it possible for universal good to emerge from partial evil. It is, then, an essential part of Pope's argument to "vindicate the ways of God to man." [6]

Since man, however, is a gregarious creature and must live with his fellow men, Epistle III (Of the Nature and State of Man with Respect to Society) attempts to show how this may be done to the best advantage of man, both as an individual and as a part of mankind. In Epistle II, Pope had emphasized self-love as the motivation for man's action. Now, in Epistle III, he demonstrates how self-love can become social love, how individual man can find personal regeneration through contributing to the whole and thus hastening the regeneration of society.

This problem of reconciling self and social love in man had troubled the early eighteenth century. It is at the base of Shaftesbury's popular Deism as expounded in *The Moralists* (1709) and in *Characteristics* (1711) and of Hobbes' social contract developed in *Leviathan* (1651). Neither solution could be termed moral. Hobbes sees man as basically unregenerate, so that only a strong, highly centralized government can keep his self-love from becoming a destructive force, productive of anarchy. Shaftesbury's Deism is little more than a form of Hedonism: man exercises his social love because to do so gives him more pleasure than indulging his self-love. Pope and Shaftesbury arrive at approximately the same conclusion, "Self-love forsook the path it first pursu'd,/And found the private in the public good" (III, 281–82). The paths which lead them to this juncture of view, however, are divergent. Pope's view of the universe is more realistic and less benevolent than Shaftesbury's; Pope accepts the supernatural element in the universe and evil as parts of an inherent reality, while Shaftesbury would reject both; and Pope's conception of moral virtue is not the easy one which lurks behind Shaftesbury's arguments.

Pope begins his discussion with a conclusion drawn from the first two epistles of the "Essay on Man":

> Here then we rest: 'The Universal Cause
> 'Acts to one end, but acts by various laws.'

. . . .
> Look round our World; behold the Chain of Love
> Combining all below and all above.   (III, 1–2, 7–8)

This "Chain of Love" is the divine law of God, or Nature, which
binds all to all. Man's assumption that he is more important than
the lower links—they exist for his sole benefit—is one of pride:
"And just as short of Reason he must fall,/Who thinks all made
for one, not one for all" (III, 47–48). Every link is mutually dependent on every other link, and each "enjoys that pow'r which
suits them best": "To bliss alike by that direction tend,/And find
the means proportion'd to their end" (III, 81–82). In the animals,
"that pow'r" is instinct; in man, it is reason. These mutually dependent links, each with its own power, create the unity of the
universe:

> God, in the nature of each being, founds
> Its proper bliss, and sets its proper bounds:
> But as he fram'd a Whole, the Whole to bless,
> On mutual Wants built mutual Happiness:
> So from the first eternal ORDER ran,
> And creature link'd to creature, man to man.
> (III, 109–14)

Because the nature of creation is unity—mutually dependent links
—the state of nature is social; and man as a part of nature must be
social:

> Nor think, in Nature's State they blindly trod;
> The state of Nature was the reign of God:
> Self-love and Social at her birth began,
> Union, the bond of all things, and of Man.   (III, 147–50)

Such amity among created things existed in the beginning, and
Pope draws a picture of that Golden Age when "Pride was not."
Man then learned from the lower orders of creation: from the
mole, he learned to plow; from the worm, to weave; from the
beasts, to use medicine; from the ant and bee, to build cities. As a
result of this communion with the lower orders, "Cities were built,
Societies were made." Man also, in his attempts to satisfy his self-

love, created marriage, family, society, and eventually government. Pope's historical sketch of the evolution of civilization is
traditional and represents the anti-primitivistic view typical of the
Augustans: the true state of nature is man at his most social and
civilized level.

The evils created by the progress of civilization resulted from
self-love: "So drives Self-love, thro' just and thro' unjust/To one
Man's pow'r, ambition, lucre, lust" (III, 269–70). But that same
selfish emotion in time forced man in his own defense to join with
others and to give up some of his liberty so that he might enjoy a
part of what he desires:

> The same Self-love, in all, becomes the cause
> Of what restrains him, Government and Laws.
> For, what one likes if others like as well,
> What serves one will, when many wills rebel?
> How shall he keep, what, sleeping or awake,
> A weaker may surprise, a stronger take?
> His safety must his liberty restrain:
> All join to guard what each desires to gain.
> Forc'd into virtue thus by Self-defence,
> Ev'n Kings learn'd justice and benevolence:
> Self-love forsook the path it first pursu'd,
> And found the private in the public good. (III, 271–82)

Thus faith and ethical principles came into man's experience:

> Man, like the gen'rous vine, supported lives;
> The strength he gains is from th'embrace he gives.
> On their own Axis as the Planets run,
> Yet make at once their circle round the Sun:
> So two consistent motions act the Soul;
> And one regards Itself, and one the Whole.
> Thus God and Nature link'd the gen'ral frame,
> And bade Self-love and Social be the same. (III, 311–18)

Private and public good, while different, are not contrary to each
other; rather, they are consistent and each mutually promotes the
other.

The theme of Epistle III is, then, again one of fall and regeneration; and, as in the first two epistles, regeneration is gained

through the reconciliation of opposites—the *discordia concors.* Self-love, when not controlled, produces anarchy or tyranny in society, religion, and government; but, when properly directed, it creates the virtue-producing balance and unity to be found in true faith and in true government. In this true state of nature man is an active, creative force for good: "all Mankind's concern is Charity" (love).

Epistle IV (Of the Nature and State of Man, with respect to Happiness) further refines the materials of the third epistle by showing that man's true happiness, or "virtue," lies in his transmuting self-love into a love of God and man. In Epistle III the emphasis was on the violation of the social order, but here it is that of the ethical order. Man, by knowing himself, accepts his place in the scheme of things (Epistle I), comes to realize the duality of his own nature and how to effect a balance of the halves (Epistle II), learns to live in accord with his fellow men by extending self-love to social love (Epistle III), and finally pushes social love into a love of all things, a benevolence which insures virtue in mankind (Epistle IV).

The irony which is implicit throughout the "Essay on Man" threatens to become open satire in Epistle IV, as Pope paints man's futile attempts to found true happiness on material values. The poem opens with a category of the sources of happiness sought by men who then discover that these are mirages: wealth, pleasure, contentment, action, ease, ambition, fame. These pursuits based on self-love cannot produce true happiness, for it comes from "thinking right, and meaning well":

> Remember, Man, 'the Universal Cause
> 'Acts not by partial, but by gen'ral laws;'
> And makes what Happiness we justly call
> Subsist not in the good of one, but all.
> There's not a blessing Individuals find,
> But some way leans and hearkens to the kind.
>   (IV, 35–40)

When man pursues material values, he is violating his own nature and denying the principle of order which is the divine law of creation. This oneness of nature is made possible by love, but it

can function only when man knows himself and through that
knowledge fulfills his proper place in the divine order:

> See! the sole bliss Heav'n could on all bestow;
> Which who but feels can taste, but thinks can know;
> Yet poor with fortune, and with learning blind,
> The bad must miss; the good, untaught, will find;
> Slave to no sect, who takes no private road,
> But looks thro' Nature, up to Nature's God;
> Pursues that Chain which links th'immense design,
> Joins heav'n and earth, and mortal and divine;
> Sees, that no being any bliss can know,
> But touches some above, and some below;
> Learns, from this union of the rising Whole,
> The first, last purpose of the human soul;
> And knows where Faith, Law, Morals, all began,
> All end, in Love of God, and Love of Man.
> For him alone, Hope leads from goal to goal,
> And opens still, and opens on his soul,
> 'Till lengthen'd on to Faith, and unconfin'd,
> It pours the bliss that fills up all the mind.
> He sees, why Nature plants in Man alone
> Hope of known bliss, and Faith in bliss unknown:
> (Nature, whose dictates to no other kind
> Are giv'n in vain, but what they seek they find)
> Wise is her present; she connects in this
> His greatest Virtue with his greatest Bliss,
> At once his own bright prospect to be blest,
> And strongest motive to assist the rest.
> Self-love thus push'd to social, to divine,
> Gives thee to make thy neighbour's blessing thine.
> Is this too little for the boundless heart?
> Extend it, let thy enemies have part:
> Grasp the whole worlds of Reason, Life, and Sense,
> In one close system of Benevolence:
> Happier as kinder, in whate'er degree,
> And height of Bliss but height of Charity. (IV, 327–60)

God "loves from Whole to Parts," but man "Must rise from Individual to the Whole": from self-love to social love, then upward to
divine love—love of the whole. This love is the "known bliss" that
man hopes for and the "unknown bliss" in which he had faith.

Having reached the conclusion of his argument, Pope closes his poem with a song to Bolingbroke, which summarizes the four epistles of the "Essay":

> Come then, my Friend, my Genius, come along,
> O master of the poet, and the song!
>
> . . . .
>
> That urg'd by thee, I turn'd the tuneful art
> From sounds to things, from fancy to the heart;
> For Wit's false mirror held up Nature's light;
> Show'd erring Pride, WHATEVER IS, IS RIGHT;
> That REASON, PASSION, answer one great aim;
> That true SELF-LOVE and SOCIAL are the same;
> That VIRTUE only makes our Bliss below;
> And all our Knowledge is, OURSELVES TO KNOW.
>
> (IV, 373–74, 391–98)

Professor Maynard Mack summarizes the "Essay on Man" in these words: "In short, the controlling theme of the *Essay on Man* as a poem is a theme of constructive renunciation. By renouncing the exterior false Paradises, man finds the true one within. By acknowledging his weaknesses, he learns his strengths. By subordinating himself to the whole, he finds his real importance in it." [7] This doctrine is the *discordia concors* once again. As one part of creation, man, in finding and fulfilling his proper place in the divine scheme of nature, contributes to the whole. The unity is made possible by the proper functioning of the many; the "friendly strife" created by the variety produces "Universal Harmony"; and love is the catalyst which binds all together.

It has been a commonplace in criticism of the "Essay on Man" to claim that the poem is a failure, either because Pope, lacking a philosophic cast of mind, could produce only a shallow philosophy, or because he does not create a philosophic system in the poem. Such a judgment is tantamount to saying that Pope's translation of the *Iliad* is a failure because he was not Homer or that the "Essay on Criticism" fails because he was not Aristotle. Such a judgment is really unfair; it results from bringing to the poem a preconceived standard of judgment which lies outside the poem itself. The application of an erroneous standard caused the Swiss theologian, Crousaz, to attack the "Essay on Man" as heterodox doctrine in 1737. Crousaz read the "Essay" not as a poem but as a religious treatise, and he read it in the faulty French translations of Silhouette (1736) and Du Resnel (1737). In examining the poem for evidence of heterodoxy, Crousaz pushed Pope's ideas further than Pope's poetry did and resolved Pope's poetic ambiguities into irreconcilable antipodes. In 1738 the poet's enemies published Crousaz' two attacks on the "Essay" and followed them with individual refutations of the separate epistles. Pope, alarmed at the situation, took comfort in Warburton's defense of the poem, published as a series of letters in the *History of the Works of the Learned.*

Although Warburton defended Pope's ideas as Christian rather than as Deistic, the true defense of the "Essay on Man" must rest on the fact that it is a poem and not a logically argued system of ethics. What Pope did was to utilize for poetic purposes ideas which passed as common ethical and moral currency in his day.[8] The "Essay" is not a logical argument, the nature of poetry not being that of logical reasoning. Pope, as a poet, is concerned more with projecting an attitude toward the ideas which are embedded in the poem than with presenting the ideas themselves. As ideas they are abstractions, and Pope clothes them with concrete details so that the reader's emotional response to them goes far beyond their intellectual content. It would be pointless and impossible to count the number of times Pope does this. One instance will suffice: Pope's impassioned attacks on man's pride cannot leave a reader unmoved or complacent, despite the reader's agreement or disagreement with Pope's treatment of pride in the rational argument. The same thing could be said about Pope's plea for the abstract principle of *discordia concors,* which is made a part of our emotional experience through copious and vivid details and illustrations. As a poem the "Essay" is full of ambiguities. To a certain degree, this ambiguity inheres in the subject matter itself. Creation in its great variety is one vast paradox of warring opposites: man is a duality of reason and emotion; human nature is wise yet foolish, virtuous yet vicious; God is fullness, yet one universal harmony. Out of these inherent ambiguities and paradoxes, the "Essay on Man" generates power as a poem.

The many poetic qualities of the "Essay" would be tedious to rehearse, and only a few of the more prominent ones must suffice:

metaphoric expression, allusion, and tone. In Epistle II, lines 25-28, Pope is discussing the neo-Platonic claim to have risen above the body.

> Or tread the mazy round his follow'rs trod,
> And quitting sense call imitating God;
> As Eastern priests in giddy circles run,
> And turn their heads to imitate the Sun.

In the last couplet quoted, Pope compares the neo-Platonists with Eastern mystics in a seemingly innocent simile. A careful reading, however, shows the lines to be rather intricate. The metaphoric comparison in the simile has actually begun with "mazy *round*" and continues building through "giddy *circles*" . . . "*turn* their heads" to its completion in "imitate the *Sun*" (the circular motions of the planets). This process of imitating God (the circle with its symbolism of perfection and eternity) by turning the head around until dizzy (as the whirling dervish does in Eastern mysticism) is like the neo-Platonic trance, wherein the soul is freed from the body; but "quitting sense" is also leaving intelligibility behind and substituting gibberish for profound comment. All this "dizziness" involved in the metaphor is to be read against the context which establishes God as order, clarity, and "Eternal Wisdom."

Pope's metaphors, however, tend to remain submerged, or unstated, unlike the simple simile quoted above. In Epistle II, lines 59–70, he discusses "Self-love" and "Reason" in a comparison with a watch (the italics are mine):

> Self-love, the *spring* of motion, acts the soul;
> Reason's comparing *balance* rules the whole.
> Man, but for that, no action could attend,
> And, but for this, were active to no end;
> Fix'd like a plant on his peculiar spot,
> To draw nutrition, propagate, and rot;
> Or, meteor-like, flame lawless thro' the void,
> Destroying others, by himself destroy'd.
>   Most strength the moving principle requires;
> Active its task, it prompts, impels, inspires.
> Sedate and quiet the comparing lies,
> Form'd but to check, delib'rate, and advise.

One cannot determine whether or not Pope was thinking of the eighteenth-century commonplace of "God the watchmaker," but his watch metaphor with the reference to "meteor-like" expands to illustrate the working of the universe itself: "self-love" is like the natural principle which keeps the planets moving while "reason" is likened by implication to the force of gravity which keeps the planets in their orbits. By using such a metaphor Pope is able to suggest that the psychological principles in the nature of man are identifiable with those natural principles which maintain order in the external universe. All (the rational, the natural, and the divine) work for one universal harmony.

Often Pope uses allusion as the equivalent of metaphor. His growth as a poet corresponds in large measure to his developing a mastery of the technique of allusion. In his later work this allusive strength becomes apparent even to a modern reader. To an eighteenth-century reader, it would have been even more obvious and would have constituted one of the chief delights in reading his poetry. The eighteenth-century poet recognized that the weaving together of the many strands of Western culture into one homogeneous fabric was his foremost obligation and glory as a poet. That Pope was well aware of this is attested by the fact that he (and later Warburton) often cited sources and authorities in footnotes to the poems. Since the stated theme of the "Essay on Man" is to "vindicate the ways of God to Man," the most obvious source of allusion is Milton's *Paradise Lost*. Oblique and direct glances at Milton are everywhere in the poem, from the opening "Garden, tempting with forbidden fruit" (I, 8) to the final lines—a paraphrase of Milton's "Be lowly wise: Think only what concerns thee and thy being" (*Paradise Lost* VIII, 173–74). These many Miltonic echoes support the central thematic similarity of the two poems: in order to learn to balance himself in a universe of good and evil man must sublimate evil so that good may eventually triumph. Milton used myth to state this theme poetically but Pope substitutes for myth the philosophic sequences of his day; still, he never reduces his poem to philosophy just as Milton never reduces *Paradise Lost* to the level of mere mythology.

Alongside the allusions from Milton are those drawn from Pope's extensive reading. Almost any verse paragraph in the poem reveals obvious as well as obscure Biblical allusions; arguments from the moral philosophers, both pagan and Christian (Cicero, Seneca, Aquinas, Montaigne, La Rochefoucauld, Pascal, Archbishop King, etc.); paraphrases from the classical and English poets (Ovid, Horace, Juvenal, Lucretius, Shakespeare, Dryden, Daniel, Sir John Davies, Donne, Prior, Thomson, etc); or echoes from writers on government, psychology, ethics, and science (Aristotle, Hobbes, Shaftesbury, Mandeville, Burton, Bacon, Chudleigh, Tillotson, Locke, etc).

Since "An Essay on Man" is a persuasive poem designed to sway men's feelings and attitudes, rhetoric plays a major role in creating its poetic texture. This rhetoric includes not only Pope's modification of time-honored patterns to create metaphoric effect but also Pope's fictive disguises as speaker in the poem. Just as one determines the attitude of a friend toward what he is saying by the tone he uses (serious, jesting, facetious, sarcastic, tender, etc.), so a poet assumes varying roles as spokesman in his poems to convey his attitude toward the statements which he makes. Without the intonation of voice to help him, the poet must rely on this disguise to convey his attitude.

In satire, the determination of tone becomes all-important to a proper understanding of the poem or to a general misunderstanding of the poem; and a general misunderstanding of this technicality had led to the erroneous portrait of Pope as a bitter little man, viciously flailing anyone who dared question his work. But Pope never speaks directly in any poem as Alexander Pope. He may speak, for example, as poet-friend, or as poet-social critic, or as poet-honest observer of vice. In the choice of tone, the relationship between the disguised poet and the person addressed is also important. When discussing the same subject, one would speak differently to an intimate friend and to a casual acquaintance; or when in anger, one would speak differently to a wife, a mother, or a father he loves. So tone (or attitude) varies, and the variation depends upon the person who speaks (poet-friend, poet-lover, poet-worshipper, etc.), the person spoken to, and the stated or implied relationship between the two. Tone, then, is the warp of a poem into which the woof is woven.

In the "Essay on Man" Pope ostensibly addresses his friend Henry St. John, Viscount Bolingbroke, a nobleman. Pope assumes a guise proper to this class and to the subject he discusses: he is

the urbane man of the world indulging in a conversation (in epistolary form) with an amateur philosopher and well-bred nobleman. While the major tone of the poem is one of urbanity, it
changes from time to time as Pope speaks in asides to his reader
(mankind); his guise shifts accordingly to that of preacher,
prophet, critic, or friend. The shifting tone maintains drama, ex-
citement, and suspense in the long conversation through four epistles. Thus Pope can range the gamut from solemn pronouncement
and wonder through hortatory passages down to scorn at presumptuous man, with the attendant parallel emotions of serenity,
indignation, and contempt. Shifts in tone are marked by compara-
ble ones in the level of language, and all are arranged so that
contrasted sections become more effective.

Although Pope spoke of the "Essay on Man" as "a *short* yet not
imperfect system of Ethics," [9] the work is a poem, not a logical
moral treatise. It is Pope's most profound poem, but it should be
read as poetry. G. Wilson Knight's advice on this matter cannot be
emphasized too strongly:

The *Essay on Man* is certainly philosophic, and yet its meaning can
only be understood in terms of its artistic structure; it is, in its own
way, one of our "musical buildings." Fundamental to all religion, art
and philosophy lies the all but insoluble problem of assimilating the
world of good and evil in man's experience to the divine powers. In the
Essay on Man we have various epistles with their own watertight ap-
proaches, at least two apparently incompatible philosophies being presented in balance, and yet we are not asked to choose one and reject
the other, but rather to accept both, and build from them a new totality. The coherence is less logical than structural, though within the
structure itself can be discovered the inmost secret of creative living, of
virtue not merely in the moral, but also in the magical, sense of that
time-honoured word. . . . It is a grand-style example of the truth
that a poet does not so much think thoughts as *make* them, though it
may be for us to attempt to think the thought which he has made. As
in a drama, where truth is shadowed by conflicting voices, so the *Essay* builds from opposition a unity. . . . After all, the philosophies
concerned are, in both instances [*i.e.,* in Shakespeare and in Pope], the
vast and general philosophies of order, hierarchy, and harmony. Such
conceptions are not the preserve of any particular age or culture,
though each in turn will naturally shape and colour them to taste. . . .
That admitted, what we have to do is to study not the official philoso-

phies, but what our poet or dramatist does with them. The danger is more insidious than it at first appears, since there is always a tendency to weight down the winged poetry, to clog its wings, with, to use Pope's impolite phrase, such "learned lumber." We must sternly avoid the temptation to explain poetry in terms of secondary rather than final causes, to reduce it to something rooted backward rather than as something pointing on. For it cannot endure enslavement to any static scheme, however vast; it is a living organism, and as such must be understood.[10]

II *"Ethic Epistles" ["Moral Essays"]*

Pope's "Moral Essays" were intended as further refinements and illustrations of the ethical system developed in general in the introductory "Essay on Man": they would treat of practical morality —"the Use of Things"—and would be included in Book II, according to the list made by Spence.[11] Pope completed four of the nine projected poems, and the history of these four poems is a tangled web spun not only by Pope to protect them and the "Essay on Man" from hostile critics but also by Warburton who added his own threads of complication.

Pope wrote at least part of the four poems concurrently with the "Essay on Man." By the end of 1731 he had completed "To Burlington" and "To Bathurst," but he published only the former on December, 1731, under the title "Of Taste," which he changed to "Of False Taste" the following month (January, 1732) when the third edition came out. Although this epistle was the first to be published, Pope placed it as Epistle IV of the "Ethic Epistles" in his collected *Works,* Volume II, in 1735. In his last revision of the poems—the suppressed "death-bed" edition of 1744, done with Warburton—Pope issued "To Burlington" as one of the "Epistles to Several Persons." [12] On his own authority as literary editor, Warburton in his 1751 edition of Pope's poetry gave the title "Moral Essays" to the four poems. Warburton's notes and rearrangement of the text show that he conceived the four poems to be expositions of moral ideas and concepts rather than poems. His title "Moral Essays" emphasizes this perversion of the poems, but the title has remained despite the fact that Pope's own choice, "Ethic Epistles," better describes their nature. The three remaining "Moral Essays" were published in the following order: "To Bathurst: of the Use of Riches" (January 15, 1733); "To Cobham:

of the Knowledge and Characters of Men" (January 16, 1734); and "To a Lady" [Martha Blount]: "of the Characters of Women" (February 8, 1735). In the 1735 collected *Works,* Pope placed the poems in a final sequence: "To Cobham," "To a Lady," "To Bathurst," and "To Burlington."

However seriously Pope may have considered the "Ethic Epistles" as *exempla* for the general thesis expounded in the "Essay on Man," one cannot help noticing the differences between the "Essay" and the four poems. For one thing, the tone of the "Epistles" is informal—more conversational and more dramatic than that of the "Essay on Man." Each "Epistle" (like a dramatic monologue of Donne) opens in the midst of an interrupted conversation, and the reader feels that he is overhearing the dialogue rather than listening to the more public, rhetorical address of "An Essay on Man."

For another thing, Pope employs in the "Epistles" the character sketch with great illustrative dexterity and for thematic purposes. The "Essay on Man" has no character sketches. The "Epistles" become a veritable picture gallery,[13] which provides satire, moral commentary, and concrete dramatic interest. The character sketch might almost be considered a contemporary creation in Pope's day, although its foundations had been laid by Aristotle's disciple Theophrastus (?–287? B.C.). The Classical tradition, possibly stimulated by characterization in the Renaissance drama, had been revived and developed in the early seventeenth century by the prose portraitists Sir Thomas Overbury, Joseph Hall, and John Earle. But it was Dryden who adapted the sketch to satiric purposes in his "Absalom and Achitophel" (1681) with such success that he never again wrote a satire without including sketches. Pope, moreover, found sketches in the satires of his beloved Horace as well as in those of Juvenal and the Restoration poets.

Pope's use of the character sketch began early in his work, the character often being generalized into a type, such as the ideal critic and his opposite in the "Essay on Criticism." There were, however, specific sketches even there: one of William Walsh in the "Essay on Criticism"; one of Sir William Trumbull in "Windsor Forest"; and the "Atticus" lines, later inserted in the "Epistle to Dr. Arbuthnot" but written as early as 1715. As his use of the sketch increased, so did the concreteness of the portraits. The hue and cry over the general sketch of "Timon" in "Of Taste" ["Epistle to Burlington"], probably convinced Pope that he could not stop readers, or enemies, from identifying the type character with an actual person, just as they had identified "Timon" with the Duke of Chandos. Since he could not avoid such identification, Pope evidently decided he might as well use names and cite actual examples of the vice being satirized; at least his letter to John Caryll of September 27, 1732, would so indicate:

My work is systematical and proceeds in order; yet that does not hinder me from finishing some of the particular parts, which may be published at any time, when I judge particular vices demand them. And I believe you'll see one or two of these next winter, one especially of the Use of Riches [*i.e.*, "To Bathurst"], which seems at present to be the favorite, nay, the only, mistress of mankind, to which all their endeavours are directed, thro' all the paths of corruption and luxury. My satire will therefore be impartial on both extremes, avarice and profusion. I shall make living examples, which inforce best, and consequently put you once more upon the defence of your friend against the roar and calumny, which I expect, and am ready to suffer in so good a cause.[14]

Also, the next epistle published, "To Bathurst" (January 15, 1733), is filled with initials for names which in the 1735 edition are spelled out. That Pope believed the effectiveness of his satire was better served by using specific characters is fully explained in two letters of July 26 and August 2, 1734, to Arbuthnot:

To attack Vices in the abstract, without touching Persons, may be safe fighting indeed, but it is fighting with Shadows. General propositions are obscure, misty, and uncertain, compar'd with plain, full, and home examples: Precepts only apply to our Reason, which in most men is but weak: Examples are pictures, and strike the Senses, nay raise the Passions, and call in those (the strongest and most general of all motives) to the aid of reformation. Every vicious man makes the case his own; and that is the only way by which such men can be affected, much less deterr'd. So that to chastise is to reform. The only sign by which I found my writings ever did any good, or had any weight, has been that they rais'd the anger of bad men. And my greatest comfort, and encouragement to proceed, has been to see, that those who have no shame, and no fear, of any thing else, have appear'd touch'd by my Satires.

I thank you dear Sir for making That your Request to me which I make my Pride, nay my Duty: "that I should continue my Disdain & Abhorrence of Vice, & manifest it still in my writings." I would indeed do it with more restrictions, & less personally; it is more agreeable to my nature, which those who know it not are greatly mistaken in: But General Satire in Times of General Vice has no force, & is no Punishment: People have ceas'd to be ashamed of it when so many are joind with them; and tis only by hunting One or two from the Herd that any Examples can be made.[15]

That Pope's contemporaries should have tried to determine the real man behind the sketch is understandable, but for scholars still to be indulging in this guessing game after two hundred years seems not only futile but foolish. Pope himself was reticent; in fact, he refused to speculate on the historicity of the characters he drew. Like characterizations in any imaginative literature, they were composites drawn with details from real persons and from imagination to meet the esthetic and satiric purposes of the specific poem in which they live. Details of any particular sketch were heightened or minimized according to the needs they served. Pope's successive revisions of the poems prove that this is true, and the feeling that Pope drew no sketches completely from life is further strengthened by the fact that few scholars agree on any one certain identification. Moreover, many of the most frequently studied characters have ancient literary prototypes stretching back to Horace and Juvenal. Although several of the portraits were sketched in isolation as particular portraits and later inserted into poems, their function in the context of the poems is what matters—not what the original purpose of the sketch was.

The "Ethic Epistles" treat of human nature, and the sketches illustrate almost every conceivable facet of it. Furthermore, they attest to the poet-speaker's insight into the nature of man. The reader trusts this speaker (Pope's *persona*) because he knows how and why people act the way they do. Such knowledge creates an aura of credibility; the poem can more easily persuade the trusting reader and thus fulfill its satiric purpose of moral reformation. But, if the character sketches in the earlier poems are incidental, those in the "Ethic Epistles" are not. They act as focal points attracting to themselves the other elements in the poem. Although the arguments of the "Epistles" are not actually subordinated to the character sketches, they so appear in the poetic impact which the poem makes: the poem springs to life as the abstract precept becomes concrete illustration in the sketches.

In Pope's final arrangement of the "Ethic Epistles," the "Epistle to Cobham" was placed first. One can readily see why Pope used "To Cobham" as an introduction to the other three poems. Its ostensible subject is man's knowledge and his character. Such a theoretical subject stands closer to the "Essay on Man," and its theory of the ruling passion as the explanation of human behavior had been treated in detail in the "Essay on Man" (II, 123–44). "To Cobham," then, is a transition from the all-inclusive theory of the "Essay on Man" to the practical applied morality of the other three "Epistles."

The argument of "To Cobham"[16] is reminiscent of the more ratiocinative passages of the "Essay on Man"; since the epistle, however, is shorter, the argument, which is necessarily more compressed, seems to dominate the poem and to damage its poetic quality. Pope opens his poem with the statement that there are two kinds of knowledge about the nature of man—that of the bookish philosopher and that derived from general observation—but both are faulty because they are based on notions and guesses (ll. 1–14). He then substantiates this conclusion by citing examples of man's vacillation which would preclude drawing any generalizations about his nature: each man has his own singular qualities; no man is stable within himself; men see things in terms of themselves; and because the mind is always in motion, it is impossible to see it clearly enough to understand it (ll. 15–40).

The mention of "action" forms the transition to the next step in the argument: action reveals the true man. Pope declares this truism to be a false assumption because action is more often dictated by emotion than reason. But granting the assumption for the sake of argument, Pope finds that one cannot distinguish important from trivial motives on the basis of action. Man judges men not by what they are but by their social class, profession, or trade (ll. 41–109). Although man may gain knowledge of the character of a few men, most men are "all things in an hour": they are inconsistent, "puzzling Contraries" (ll. 110–35). At this point the poem comes to life as Pope illustrates the unpredictable nature of man with character sketches of Catius, the epicure, and of Patritio, the honest patriot. The conclusion drawn from these precepts and examples is that opinion of man's character is not a sufficient guide to knowledge of it; therefore, such knowledge must rest on something in man which is changeless (ll. 154–73).

The only stable element in man is his ruling passion because man's behavior is consistent with his particular ruling passion:

> Search then the Ruling Passion: There, alone,
> The Wild are constant, and the Cunning known;
> The Fool consistent, and the False sincere;
> Priests, Princes, Women, no dissemblers here.
> This clue once found, unravels all the rest
> . . . .   (ll. 174–78)

This thesis is then illustrated by the full-length portrait (the only one in the poem) of Wharton,[17] "Whose ruling Passion was the Lust of Praise" (ll. 178–227). Pope then concludes "To Cobham" with the statement that the ruling passion is not even affected by time. This statement brings forth, in a burst of poetic brilliance, seven short sketches of people caught at the very moment of death, still gripped by their ruling passions (ll. 228–61). The seven sketches are almost caricatures, but Pope's pen etches them with such deftness that they remain in the reader's memory. The character of Helluo, the glutton, illustrates the quality of the other six:

> A salmon's belly, Helluo, was thy fate,
> The doctor call'd, declares all help too late.
> Mercy! cries Helluo, mercy on my soul!
> Is there no hope? Alas!—then bring the jowl.   (ll. 234–37)

The portraits of the seven foolish people are balanced by a short sketch of wise Cobham, whose ruling passion is his love of England.

For all of the poem's abstract argument and theorizing about the ruling passion, one feels that Pope's real theme is the nature of reality and unreality (men are not what they seem: the mystery of human nature is ultimately unfathomable). At times this theme is presented by direct satire as in the seven portraits; at others, it

lurks beneath the surface of an exquisite irony as in these lines
which suggest that we judge a man's character by his social position:

> 'Tis from high Life high Characters are drawn;
> A saint in Crape is twice a Saint in Lawn;
> A Judge is just, a Chanc'lor juster still;
> A Gownman, learn'd; a Bishop, what you will;
> Wise, if a Minister; but, if a King,
> More wise, more learn'd, more just, more ev'rything.
> Court-virtues bear, like Gems, the highest rate,
> Born where Heav'n's influence scarce can penetrate:
> In life's low vale, the soil the virtues like,
> They please as Beauties, here as Wonders strike.
> Tho' the same Sun with all-diffusive rays
> Blush in the Rose, and in the Diamond Blaze,
> We prize the stronger effort of his pow'r,
> And justly set the Gem above the Flow'r.   (ll. 87–100)

"Ethic Epistle II: To a Lady" has been lauded as one of Pope's
masterpieces. Like "To Cobham," "To a Lady" treats of the complexity of human nature, but this time "Of the Characters of
Women" rather than those of men. There were characterizations
of women in "To Cobham," a fact which indicates that the epistle
had dealt with mankind and not only the male members of the
human family. "To a Lady," however, treats only feminine human
nature.[18] The characters of women are as transient as those of
men; in fact, they are more so because the female temperament is
by its nature more subject to vagary than that of the male. The
"Epistle" opens on this idea, for Pope quotes an old maxim, which
he claims the lady once had observed: "Nothing so true as what
you once let fall,/ 'Most Women have no Characters at all'" (ll.
1–2).

To a modern reader the line may seem satiric, even insulting to
Martha Blount; but Pope is distinguishing between man and
woman on the basis of the psychology current in his day. The
male has "character" because he is the rational, active force; the
female has sensibility, or intuition, and is the passive force. Milton's Adam and Eve were depicted in like manner:

> . . . for in their looks divine
> The image of their glorious maker shone,
>
> · · · · · · · · · · · · · ·
>
> . . . though both
> Not equal, as their sex not equal seemed;
> For contemplation he and valor formed,
> For softness she and sweet attractive grace,
> He for God only, she for God in him.
>
> (*Paradise Lost* IV, 291–92, 295–99)

To illustrate this variety and transitory quality of the female character, Pope draws six successive portraits of one woman; and each picture represents a different phase of the shifting feminine sensibility. The series is done in imagery which suggests the fragility and insubstantiality of such "character": "Cynthia" (the moon), "Cloud," "fall," "change," "catch," "minute," and "rainbow."

Since these six views are portraits, Pope introduces a painting metaphor, which runs throughout the whole poem:

> Pictures like these, dear Madam, to design
> Asks no firm hand, and no unerring line;
> Some wond'ring touches, some reflected light,
> Some flying stroke alone can hit 'em right:
> For how should equal Colours do the knack?
> Chameleons who can paint in white and black?
>
> · · · · · · · · · · · · · · · ·
>
> One certain Portrait may (I grant) be seen,
> Which Heav'n has varnish'd out, and made a *Queen:*
> The same for ever! and describ'd by all
> With Truth and Goodness, as with Crown and Ball.
> Poets heap Virtues, Painters Gems at will,
> And show their zeal, and hide their want of skill.
> 'Tis well—but, Artists! who can paint or write,
> To draw the Naked is your true delight.
> That Robe of Quality so struts and swells,
> None see what Parts of Nature it conceals.
>
> (ll. 150–56, 181–92)

This structural metaphor functions as a symbol to suggest the theme of "To a Lady," a theme which is larger than the ostensible one concerning the transience of the female character. Professor Maynard Mack sums it up in the following way:

The metaphor of the painter is kept alive throughout most of the poem because it also underscores this theme. The reason these portraits are hard to paint, the poet admits, is that their subjects change so fast; and their changeableness of mood is only a reflection of a deeper law of change: "Still round and round the Ghosts of Beauty glide." "Painting," therefore, gradually deepens in the poem from a pleasant way of imaging the delicate variegations of female temperaments to a very profound image for what is the matter with this world: it lives like painting—like the symbolic woman of the opening lines who is merely a succession of "paintings"—in appearances, in surfaces, in pose. For this reason, when the poet comes to speak of the ideal woman, he drops the painting figure and turns aside from the imaginary gallery to the living woman beside him with whom he has been discussing it. In *her* he can depict the ideal because she is *real:* she does not live in a world of surfaces—and so is not a creation of canvas and paint.[19]

Pope was quite knowledgeable about painting. In 1713 he had studied the art with the portrait painter Charles Jervas, and one or two of Pope's paintings still survive. Technical terms and similes drawn from painting are evident in his poetry, but attempts to prove any direct influence of the art on his poems have not been conclusive.[20] Pope doubtless subscribed in general to Horace's theory that *poesis ut pictura* ("Poetry resembles painting"), but he was too fine a poetic craftsman not to realize that the methods of the two arts differ greatly.

Pope's method in "To a Lady" differs from that of "To Cobham." In the latter a seemingly logical argument is illustrated by character sketches; the reverse is true in "To a Lady." The ethical significance of the poem emerges from the rapid succession of the portraits. At first glance, the reader is fascinated but slightly confused by the great variety of women portrayed—the witty, the silly, the cunning, the soft-natured, the affected, the refined, the frail—Rufa, Sappho, Silia, Papillia, Calista, Narcissa, Philomede, Flavia, Atossa, Cloë. From the seemingly inexhaustible gallery, the reader begins to realize the subtle theme of the poem—human nature in woman, as in man, is inscrutable; it is as variable as the clothes women wear.

In addition to creating the feeling of the theme of the poem, "Woman's at best a Contradiction still," these sketches lead to a generalization about womankind; and they serve as a contrast to the final sketch—a gallant, courtly portrait of Martha Blount to whom the "Epistle" is addressed. The generalization toward which the portraits work is a distinction between men and women in terms of the ruling passion:

> In Men, we various Ruling Passions find,
> In Women, two almost divide the kind;
> Those, only fix'd, they first or last obey,
> The Love of Pleasure, and the Love of Sway.
>   That, Nature gives; and when the lesson taught
> Is but to please, can Pleasure seem a fault?
> Experience, this; by Man's Oppression curst,
> They seek the second not to lose the first.
>   Men, some to Bus'ness, some to Pleasure take;
> But ev'ry Woman is at heart a Rake;
> Men, some to Quiet, some to public Strife;
> But ev'ry Lady would be Queen for life.   (ll. 207–18)

The ethical significance of this distinction is driven home with an almost savage satire:

> At last, to follies Youth could scarce defend,
> It grows their Age's prudence to pretend;
> Asham'd to own they gave delight before,
> Reduc'd to feign it, when they give no more:
> As Hags hold Sabbaths, less for joy then spight,
> So these their merry, miserable Night;
> Still round and round the Ghosts of Beauty glide,
> And haunt the places where their Honour dy'd.
>   See how the World its Veterans rewards!
> A Youth of frolicks, an old Age of Cards,
> Fair to no purpose, artful to no end,
> Young without Lovers, old without a Friend,
> A Fop their Passion, but their Prize a Sot,
> Alive, ridiculous, and dead, forgot!   (ll. 235–48)

In contrast to this horrible depiction of vanity's old age and the many preceding sketches which illustrate it, comes the address to Martha Blount:

> Ah Friend! to dazzle let the Vain design,
> To raise the Thought and touch the Heart, be thine!
>
> . . . .
> Heav'n, when it strives to polish all it can

Its last best work, but forms a softer Man;
Picks from each sex, to make the Fav'rite blest,
Your love of Pleasure, our desire of Rest,
Blends, in exception to all gen'ral rules,
Your taste of Follies, with our Scorn of Fools,
Reserve with Frankness, Art with Truth ally'd,
Courage with Softness, Modesty with Pride,
Fix'd Principles, with Fancy ever new;
Shakes all together, and produces—You.
 Be this a Woman's Fame: with this unblest,
Toasts live a scorn, and Queens may die a jest.
This Phoebus promis'd (I forget the year)
When those blue eyes first open'd on the sphere;
Ascendant Phoebus watch'd that hour with care,
Averted half your Parents simple Pray'r,
And gave you Beauty, but deny'd the Pelf
That buys your sex a Tyrant o'er itself.
The gen'rous God, who Wit and Gold refines,
And ripens Spirits as he ripens Mines,
Kept Dross for Duchesses, the world shall know it,
To you gave Sense, Good-humour, and a Poet.
                    (ll. 249–50, 271–92)

The positive quality in the lines about Patty Blount makes them different from the preceding character sketches, in all of which there inheres a negative force rather than a positive one. In Atossa, this negative quality is violent rage, which produces nothing; in Philomede, it is lust, which is sterile; in Flavia, it is wit which dies "of nothing but a Rage to live"; in Cloë, it is a lack of human feeling. In contrast to them is Martha Blount with her reserve, truthfulness, courage, modesty, resoluteness, imagination, good sense, and good humor. These moral values spring from a positive creative force. They are the same womanly virtues which Pope had extolled years before in the "Rape of the Lock."

The third "Ethic Epistle" is devoted to the subject of the use of riches; the practical morality of the poem derives from its picture of the effect money has on society and its examination of the discrepancies between monetary values and moral values. This basic discrepancy is explored in terms of nature; the individual man; man as participant in society, friendship, charity, and economic theory; and man as the inheritor of good and evil. The verse letter is addressed to Lord Bathurst,[21] a man of the world. Perhaps Bathurst's contemporary reputation as a man of loose morals explains one of the major tones of the poem—that of the cynical, worldly man.

As Professor Wasserman points out, tone—which is always important in Pope's poetry—is most complex in "To Bathurst." In this poem the attitudes expressed are extremely complicated because the satire is not limited to any one area: it is "the whole corruptness of the new moneyed society he [Pope] sees mushrooming about him and invading his values." [22] The problem of tone is related to the form of the poem. On the 31st of January, 1733, Pope wrote to John Caryll referring to the "Epistle" as a sermon: "You live daily in my thoughts, and sometimes in my prayers, if you will let a poet talk of prayers. Yet at least I have some title to *sermons,* which are next of kin to prayers. I find the last I made [*i.e.,* "To Bathurst"] had some good effect, and yet the preacher less railed at than usually those are who will be declaiming against popular or national vices. I shall redouble my blow very speedily." [23]

Pope uses the term "sermon" in its Horatian meaning of *sermo* —satire to effect reformation. The "epistle" is, then, Horatian satire, which would represent virtue by exposing vice—in this instance, the vice of the misuse of money, with the proper use of money often stated and always implied. The rapidly increasing wealth of the urban, upper middle class was threatening the older social order of the landed gentry of which Bathurst was a member. The South Sea Company debacle, in which Pope had lost money, was in the immediate background of the poem and doubtless was proof to Pope of the perversion of the older standard of values. Pope's "Epistle," like all satire, is conservative in that it attempts to exalt an older, more stable system of values; but this is not to say that the older system of values is claimed to be synonymous with the older *status quo,* for the very reason that satire is progressive while it at the same time urges conservatism. Such a purpose would be in keeping with the Augustan concept of the Horatian *sermo.*

But the rhetorical development of the poem shows that Pope uses the term also in its Christian sense of "homily." Bathurst is named a follower of Momus (line 3) and is described as a cynical, pagan philosopher, who believes "That Man was made the standing jest of Heav'n/And Gold but sent to keep the fools in play" (ll. 4–5). Bathurst's *persona,* then, is the classical, witty, sophisticated, philosophic man of the world. Pope's *persona* is that of the lay Christian: "But I, who think more highly of our kind,/ (And surely, Heav'n and I are of a mind)" (ll. 7–8). In this manner, Pope establishes a contrast between the two speakers, each maintaining his own point of view.

But, as Professor Wasserman clearly proves, Pope wants more than a contrast. By the use of ingenious rhetorical devices and rich allusions to Scripture and Christian literature, Pope forces pagan philosopher Bathurst to accept the argument proposed on the grounds of the lay theologian. By such a shift, Pope creates two important concerns for his "Epistle." For one thing, the fusion of the Christian and Classical ideas gives the poem a richness of allusive texture, which is almost inexhaustible, and thus makes possible satiric thrusts on several levels of meaning and emotional response simultaneously. Moreover, as the speaker continues to lead Bathurst into successive Christian points of view concerning wealth and its use, Bathurst's shift in position—in conceding the lay Christian's argument—moves the poem from the realm of worldly ethics to that of Christian morals.

Bathurst's opening comment (given in indirect discourse by the speaker) is that man is a contemptible, trivial creature, the "standing jest of Heav'n"; but this judgment is countered by the speaker's view of the word "standing." Man, alone of all creatures, *stands* upright and thus reaches toward Heaven. This fact, according to Christian symbolism, proves that the human being is superior to the rest of creation: man is a spiritual entity as well as a physical one. The force of this argument is felt when the word "Gold," introduced in the next line, is thereafter developed by reference to a series of economic ideas and points of view, both worldly and Christian. The worldly philosopher and the lay Christian agree that the possession of wealth indicates

> No grace of Heav'n or token of th' Elect;
> Giv'n to the Fool, the Mad, the Vain, the Evil,
> To Ward, to Waters, Chartres, and the Devil.   (ll. 18–20)

In other words, gold is a phenomenon of nature. The value set upon it is man-made and not divine, despite the Calvinistic claim that God prospers the elected good man. Gold is given to the "Fool, the Mad, the Vain"; and even the "Devil" misuses it, as is evident in the cases of John Ward, Peter Waters, and Francis Chartres, profligate rakes who garnered ill-gotten fortunes.

Divine nature, in order to counteract "Man's audacious labour" in finding gold and placing such value on it, divided men into opposing groups—the wastrels and the misers. This opposition had been foreshadowed at the opening of the poem by the contrasted pagan and Christian views of man, which are then accommodated to each other. In like manner, these extremes of spendthrift and miser are also resolved later in the poem when the moral values involved with wealth are introduced and the virtuous use of money is detailed. These extremes also allow Pope to make extensive satiric comment on luxury (the wastrel's use of money) and avarice (how the miser uses it).

Pope's speaker maneuvers his philosophic opponent into the admission that in the world of fallen mankind the use of money makes gold either good or bad:

> Since then, my Lord, on such a World we fall,
> What say you? "Say? Why take it, Gold, and all."
> What Riches give us let us then enquire,
> Meat, Fire, and Cloaths. What more? Meat, Cloaths, and
> Fire.
> Is this too little? would you more than live? (ll. 79–83)

The corruption of man by wealth alone is proof of the "Fallen" human condition which all men share. The lines quoted indicate that the problem is not gold in itself but the moral obligations which wealth places on those who have it. Obviously, gold is necessary to supply the basic human needs of "Meat, Fire, and Cloaths." This necessity is recognized by Christian teaching; but Christian doctrine also poses the question of line 101: "Perhaps you think the Poor might have their part?" Charity is basic to Christianity, and the proper use of money becomes a Christian moral obligation as the lay theologian's voice damns the directors of the Charitable Corporation for the Relief of the Industrious

Poor, the speculator-financiers of the South Sea Company and Walpole's Whig economic policies.

As the speaker's voice grows more indignant, the imagery of finance becomes more and more identified with evil. In a bursting torrent of rhetoric, the voice of righteous indignation sweeps all before it and plunges into a prophetic indictment of a nation which tolerates such immoral use of wealth:

> 'At length Corruption, like a gen'ral flood,
> '(So long by watchful Ministers withstood)
> 'Shall deluge all; and Av'rice creeping on,
> 'Spread like a low-born mist, and blot the Sun;
> 'Statesman and Patriot ply alike the stocks,
> 'Peeress and Butler share alike the Box,
> 'And Judges job, and Bishops bite the town,
> 'And mighty Dukes pack cards for half a crown.
> 'See Britain sunk in lucre's sordid charms,
> 'And France revenged of Anne's and Edward's arms!'
> 'Twas no Court-badge, great Scrib'ner! fir'd thy brain,
> Nor lordly Luxury, nor City Gain:
> No, 'twas thy righteous end, asham'd to see
> Senates degen'rate, Patriots disagree,
> And nobly wishing Party-rage to cease,
> To buy both sides, and give thy Country peace. (ll. 137–52)

The answer to this situation and to the problem of wealth postulated early in the poem follows the prophetic outburst:

> Hear then the truth: ' 'Tis Heav'n each Passion sends,
> 'And diff'rent men directs to diff'rent ends.
> 'Extremes in Nature equal good produce,
> 'Extremes in Man concur to gen'ral use.'
> Ask we what makes one keep, and one bestow?
> That Pow'r who bids the Ocean ebb and flow,
> Bids seed-time, harvest, equal course maintain,
> Thro' reconcil'd extremes of drought and rain,
> Builds Life on Death, on Change Duration founds,
> And gives th' eternal wheels to know their rounds. (ll. 161–70)

This doctrine of "reconcil'd extremes" offers a solution, not in an ideal state of existence, but in this real "fallen" world. The state of reconciled extremes is the true state of moral virtue, not a statement of Mandevillian economics. Divine providence in its infinite wisdom creates the prodigal man and the miser. Man, however, is still responsible and obliged to seek perfection; but, since man cannot attain total perfection, providence reconciles the extremes which men create out of themselves and thus fulfills its divine purpose and harmony in individual men, just as it fulfills cosmic harmony through *discordia concors*.

Pope's solution is close to Aristotle's definition of virtue as the mean between two extremes; thus, the character sketches of the two Cottas, father and son (ll. 179–218), illuminate this virtue as the mean between prodigality and miserliness. The two Cottas, however, illustrate the point negatively: they both fail to find the mean between the extremes. The son, trying to avoid the father's extreme of niggardliness, "mistook reverse of wrong for right" and ended his life a bankrupt out of zeal for England. Even his well-intentioned motive for prodigality proved no virtue.

In contrast to the Cottas, Bathurst himself is an illustration of the Aristotelian virtuous man, at least as far as wealth is concerned.

> The Sense to value Riches, with the Art
> T'enjoy them, and the Virtue to impart,
> Not meanly, nor ambitiously pursu'd,
> Not sunk by sloth, nor rais'd by servitude;
> To balance Fortune by a just expence,
> Join with OEconomy, Magnificence;
> With splendour, charity, with plenty, health;
> Oh teach us, BATHURST! yet unspoil'd by wealth!
> That secret rare, between th' extremes to move
> Of mad Good-nature, and of mean Self-love.   (ll. 219–28)

Bathurst's virtue, however, is of a Classical (Aristotelian), ethical nature in keeping with his *persona* established early in the poem; it is not that of the Christian. A third illustration of this kind of virtue, in the Man of Ross, raises the Classical, ethical virtue to a level of Christian moral principle. In this character sketch, the Man of Ross (ll. 250–90) preserves the Aristotelian virtue, but his Christ-like nature, implied in the allusions and imagery, indicates that his virtue constitutes the perfection fallen man can attain.

Although the portrait of the Man of Ross ends Pope's line of

argument, the artistic structure of the poem is concluded by a
series of lesser sketches which analyze the theme of the "Epistle":
"No man can serve God and Mammon." Professor Wasserman's
close study of the portraits shows that Pope carefully balanced
them: they are positive, creative, and good—or they are negative,
destructive, and evil. Buckingham (ll. 299–314) is an *exemplum*
of the end of prodigality as is Cutler (ll. 315–34) the end of miserliness; both balance the two Cottas. All of them, as illustrative of a
negative and destructive force, are in contrast to the Man of Ross,
the positive, creative force and, to a lesser degree, to Bathurst,
whose pagan ethics are nonetheless creative. That the Man of
Ross' use of wealth is in agreement with the creative impulse of
nature is reinforced by the pastoral setting of his sketch, a setting
which is mythic and traditionally associated with the Golden Age:

> Rise, honest Muse! and sing the Man of Ross:
> Pleas'd Vaga echoes thro' her winding bounds,
> And rapid Severn hoarse applause resounds.
> Who hung with woods yon mountain's sultry brow?
> From the dry rock who bade the waters flow?   (ll. 250–54)

As a dweller in the countryside, he is also in contrast to the urban
Balaam of the financial heart of the city. The Man of Ross consciously uses his money to enrich nature and to help further her
simple plan. The economic cycle created by his use of his material
goods is analogous to the rhythmic cycles of nature. In the Man of
Ross, man and nature are in agreement; he is, therefore, a pattern
for individual and social regeneration.

The climax of the poem is reached in the concluding sketch of
Sir Balaam (ll. 339–402), who combines the individual evils of all
the other negative portraits. It is one of Pope's most damning
drawings and one of his most richly allusive. The imagery identifies Sir Balaam generically with Satan, Sir Robert Walpole and
the Whig politico-economic immorality, Calvinistic economic doctrine, and the corruption of moral and social values by the urban
control of wealth.

The "Epistle to Bathurst" has long been treated as one of Pope's
less successful and uncongenial poems, but Professor Wasserman
has shown that this evaluation is incorrect. He further argues that

the "Epistle to Bathurst" and the fourth "Ethic Epistle"—the one
addressed to the Earl of Burlington—present Pope's mature views
on the "Use of Riches." He sees the two epistles as "Pope's satiric
adaptation of Aristotle's analysis of the ethics of wealth." [24] Aristotle's *Nicomachean Ethics* presented the idea of two virtues in
the use of riches: liberality and magnificence. The two differ in
degree rather than in kind. Liberality is the mean—the point half-
way between waste and miserliness. This virtue would be applicable to most human beings, whether their wealth be great or modest. Magnificence, however, is applicable only to large amounts of
wealth; magnificence is the mean between vulgarity and shabbiness. Aristotle further defines vulgarity as the application of great
things to inappropriate objects, a definition which Pope illustrates
in the following couplet from "Burlington": "Load some vain
Church with old Theatric state,/Turn Arcs of triumph to a
Garden-gate" (ll. 29–30). Magnificence, then, is more closely related to taste than is liberality. The latter is more involved with
moral value than is magnificence. Aristotle gives magnificence an
ethical value in that he declares a preference for vulgar display
over shabbiness caused by parsimoniousness; someone benefits
from prodigality but no one from niggardliness. Pope states this
idea in lines 169–72:

> Yet hence the Poor are cloath'd, the Hungry fed;
> Health to himself, and to his Infants bread
> The Lab'rer bears: what his hard Heart denies,
> His charitable Vanity supplies.

Pope goes further than Aristotle in relating magnificence to moral
values. On the basis of these definitions, Professor Wasserman di-
vides the two epistles on the use of riches into a sermon on liberality ("To Bathurst") and one on magnificence ("To Burlington").

Since "To Bathurst" is more concerned with the moral problems
of proper charity than is "To Burlington," Pope's tone in the former is quite appropriately that of the lay theologian. In "To Burlington," [25] where the problem is more one of good taste than
moral values (although they are never absent), Pope's tone is that
of the aristocratic, highly civilized gentleman of the Augustan era.
In fact, Pope's *persona* might well be a man from the Rome of

Caesar Augustus, that high point of impeccable good taste for the
Augustan gentleman. Reuben Brower notes that Pope's ironic tone
is maintained by more or less "direct allusion to the Roman achieve-
ment and an ideal civilization," which, in turn, is supported by the
paraphernalia of ancient culture ("Temples and a Hecatomb," l.
156); by parody of the Classical styles of heroic, pastoral, and
elegiac; and by ancient architecture and religious ceremonies that
are degraded by modern vulgarity.[26] Also, since the dramatic *persona* who speaks in the poem governs the attitudes expressed in it,
Pope achieves his ironic tone by posing as the cultured, tasteful,
Roman gentleman who is surveying the vulgar effects of eighteenth-century wealth on architecture, gardening, and the social
amenities.

The opening lines of the "Epistle to Burlington" suggest not
only its relationship to "Bathurst" but also the problem of taste
that is its primary concern:

> 'Tis strange, the Miser should his Cares employ,
> To gain those Riches he can ne'er enjoy:
> Is it less strange, the Prodigal should waste
> His wealth, to purchase what he ne'er can taste?
> Not for himself he sees, or hears, or eats;
> Artists must choose his Pictures, Music, Meats:
> He buys for Topham, Drawings and Designs,
> For Pembroke, Statues, dirty Gods, and Coins;
> Rare monkish Manuscripts for Hearne alone,
> And Books for Mead, and Butterflies for Sloane.
> Think we all these are for himself? no more
> Than his fine Wife, alas! or finer Whore.   (ll. 1–12)

Pope's explication of bad taste is somewhat complex in its interre-
lationships with nature, social and individual behavior, and moral
values. The basis of good taste resides in nature: the proper ex-
penditure of wealth with true taste to produce magnificence never
violates the natural principles of order and utility. False taste imitates not nature but copies of it:

> Yet shall (my Lord) your just, your noble rules
> Fill half the land with Imitating Fools;
> Who random drawings from your sheets shall take,
> And of one beauty many blunders make;

. . . .

> Conscious they act a true Palladian part,
> And, if they starve, they starve by rules of art.
>
> (ll. 25–28, 37–38)

Good taste, however, is something which cannot be bought with riches:

> Oft have you hinted to your brother Peer,
> A certain truth, which many buy too dear:
> Something there is more needful than Expence,
> And something previous ev'n to Taste—'tis Sense:
> Good Sense, which only is the gift of Heav'n,
> And tho' no science, fairly worth the seven:
> A Light, which in yourself you must perceive;
> Jones and Le Notre have it not to give.
> To build, to plant, whatever you intend,
> To rear the Column, or the Arch to bend,
> To swell the Terras, or to sink the Grot;
> In all, let Nature never be forgot.
> But treat the Goddess like a modest fair,
> Nor over-dress, nor leave her wholly bare;
> Let not each beauty ev'ry where be spy'd,
> Where half the skill is decently to hide.
> He gains all points, who pleasingly confounds,
> Surprizes, varies, and conceals the Bounds.
> Consult the Genius of the Place in all;
> That tells the Waters or to rise, or fall,
> Or helps th' ambitious Hill the heav'ns to scale,
> Or scoops in circling theatres the Vale,
> Calls in the Country, catches opening glades,
> Joins willing woods, and varies shades from shades,
> Now breaks, or now directs, th' intending Lines;
> Paints as you plant, and, as you work, designs.
> Still follow Sense, of ev'ry Art the Soul,
> Parts answ'ring parts shall slide into a whole,
> Spontaneous beauties all around advance,
> Start ev'n from Difficulty, strike from Chance;
> Nature shall join you, Time shall make it grow
> A Work to wonder at—perhaps a Stow.   (ll. 39–70)

To follow nature truly, which is good taste, includes, first of all, "Good Sense" (l. 43), a quality derived partly from education (equal to the seven liberal arts) and partly from inherent instinct

—somewhat akin to the religious "inner light" (1. 45). Second, to follow nature is to respect "propriety," whose standards are derived from the designs of nature: water runs downhill, fields join with woods, and hills rise toward heaven. But "propriety" relates as well to individual and social behavior, and good taste requires good morals on the part of man if he is not to offend nature. Thus, while "Burlington" is cast in a minor moral key compared to "Bathurst," the moral implications are always visible beneath the surface of the poem. Third, to follow nature with good taste one must expend his wealth in a useful way:

> Who then shall grace, or who improve the Soil?
> Who plants like Bathurst, or who builds like Boyle.
> 'Tis Use alone that sanctifies Expence,
> And Splendour borrows all her rays from Sense. (ll. 177–80)

Unlike the "Epistle to Bathurst" with its galaxy of portraits, the "Epistle to Burlington" has only one stellar sketch—that of "Timon." It is the *exemplum* of bad taste, of vulgarity (ll. 99–168); and Pope has lavished attention on its every detail. Timon himself is not an evil man, but his villa and way of life violate every principle of nature, good taste, and usefulness. His sense of values is in keeping with the pretentiousness of his estate: all exists "to be seen" (1. 128). Timon values age and rareness in books but not their contents or authors; he believes that size indicates worth:

> Greatness, with Timon, dwells in such a draught
> As brings all Brobdingnag before your thought.
> To compass this, his building is a Town,
> His pond an Ocean, his parterre a Down:
> Who but must laugh, the Master when he sees,
> A puny insect, shiv'ring at a breeze! (ll. 103–8)

Timon does not realize that he is dwarfed into "A puny insect" by the expanse of his surroundings. He and his guests are made uncomfortable by the environment because his poor taste has violated nature: the largeness of his pond causes him and his guests to shiver "at a breeze" or to burn in a "Summer-house, that knows no shade." A meal in the dining room is an ordeal:

> But hark! the chiming Clocks to dinner call;
> A hundred footsteps scrape the marble Hall:
> The rich Buffet well-colour'd Serpents grace,
> And gaping Tritons spew to wash your face.
> Is this a dinner? this a Genial room?
> No, 'tis a Temple, and a Hecatomb.
> A solemn Sacrifice, perform'd in state,
> You drink by measure, and to minutes eat.
> So quick retires each flying course, you'd swear
> Sancho's dread Doctor and his Wand were there.
> Between each Act the trembling salvers ring,
> From soup to sweet-wine, and God bless the King.
> In plenty starving, tantaliz'd in state,
> And complaisantly help'd to all I hate.   (ll. 151–64)

The meal is not a relaxed pleasure; it is as formal as a religious ceremony, which the imagery implies; and the incongruity which ensues from the imagery is an illustration of the definition of vulgarity: the application of the wrong values to inappropriate objects. The same thing is true of Timon's chapel, which ironically offers the ease lacking in the dining room:

> And now the Chapel's silver bell you hear,
> That summons you to all the Pride of Pray'r:
> Light quirks of Musick, broken and uneven,
> Make the soul dance upon a Jig to Heaven.
> On painted Ceilings you devoutly stare,
> Where sprawl the Saints of Verrio or Laguerre,
> On gilded clouds in fair expansion lie,
> And bring all Paradise before your eye.
> To rest, the Cushion and soft Dean invite,
> Who never mentions Hell to ears polite.   (ll. 141–50)

Timon's gardens further illustrate his offenses against nature, or good taste:

> His Gardens next your admiration call,
> On ev'ry side you look, behold the Wall!
> No pleasing Intricacies intervene,
> No artful wildness to perplex the scene;
> Grove nods at grove, each Alley has a brother,

> And half the platform just reflects the other.
> The suff'ring eye inverted Nature sees,
> Trees cut to Statues, Statues thick as trees,
> With here a Fountain, never to be play'd,
> And there a Summer-house, that knows no shade.
>   (ll. 113–22)

But nature is eternal, and Timon's offenses against it cannot endure:

> Another age shall see the golden Ear
> Imbrown the Slope, and nod on the Parterre,
> Deep Harvests bury all his pride has plann'd,
> And laughing Ceres re-assume the land.   (ll. 173–76)

These lines contain the ideological and emotional climax of the poem. Man's life and work must be in accord with the principles of nature if they are to endure and to have moral value. Expressed again is Pope's belief in the divine harmony of all creation, a harmony which can also be achieved by man if he will follow nature's designs and conform his life to them. One man who has done this, Pope feels, is Burlington; and the "Epistle" closes with a formal, rhetorical passage which exhorts Burlington to continue his works of magnificence and thus become a pattern to England and its rulers in their attempts to build a greater nation.

This insistence on harmony between man and nature might be considered the theme of the total ethical system which Pope had originally projected in the five poems here considered. The "Essay on Man" presents man as if in the abstract, and the four "Ethic Epistles" present him in the particular. In the "Essay," man's pride causes him to break his union with external nature (Epistle I), with his own inner nature (Epistle II), and with his social nature, that is, his relationship with his fellow human beings (Epistle III); and, as a result of these violations, man is unhappy in his ethical relationships (Epistle IV). But the argument of the "Essay on Man," when reduced to a prose summary such as this, seems to present a negative approach and will be unjust to Pope. The "Essay" and the four "Ethic Epistles" are positive, not negative. Pope uses every poetic means in his power to proclaim the creative force of man and nature reconciled. Man does not passively accept nature; he affirmatively works with nature and thus both become creative forces. Virtue, in the fourth epistle of "An Essay on Man," is not a withdrawal or an abstaining from the world. Pope, like Milton, would never "praise a fugitive and cloistered virtue unexercised and unbreathed." Man must "know himself," and through that knowledge fulfill the divine order in universal nature, human nature, social nature, and ethical nature. Each is a part of the other, and the whole can function properly only when each does its part.

The "Ethic Epistles" present the same view of man as a positive, creative force when he works in accord with nature. Throughout the stress is on persons who work with nature and those who violate nature's accord. Time and again, the character sketches emphasize that negativism or passiveness is self-defeating and destructive; living in accord with nature is creative, whether in the individual, the social, or the moral realm. Nature is eternal; it is divine order. And man must reconcile the extremes of his nature and must live in agreement with the principles of total nature if he is to be a whole being, physically, socially, and morally.

In their emphasis on the potentiality of man's becoming a creative force when in accord with nature, the five poems are Pope's last wholeheartedly optimistic view of man and society. Within the poems themselves, however, one sees the growth of a more tragic view of life. The satire of "An Essay on Man" remains generalized, directed against pride, a sin common to all mankind. In the "Ethic Epistles," the satire becomes more specific and biting as Pope singles out types of human beings who violate the harmony of nature. In "To a Lady"—chronologically the last of these epistles—his pity and his bitterness at the spectacle of humankind approach the unendurable. At moments, Pope's insight into the weakness of man seems to leave him with little hope for improvement. This darker view of life predominates in the Horatian imitations that he wrote after abandoning the ethical system. Perhaps this weakening of his optimism was a factor in his decision not to complete the system which was to "make mankind look upon this life with comfort and pleasure, and put morality in good humour." [27]

CHAPTER 4

The Augustan Horace

FROM 1733 to 1738 Pope was occupied in writing seventeen poems in imitation of or in the spirit of Horace. These poems not only follow as a group the five which comprise Pope's ethical system but they are also related to the earlier poems in several ways. For one thing, the projected system of ethics was to treat "Of the Principles and Use of Civil Polity." No such subject was eventually covered in the "moral scheme," but several of the Horatian imitations discuss contemporary abuses of the principles of true government. It is likely that Pope, upon abandoning his original plan and being reluctant to discard any ideas or lines already written, used the old material in his newly cast poetic form—the Horatian imitation. For another thing, the increasing use of the character sketch in the "Ethic Epistles" is carried to its satiric fulfillment in the Horatian poems which are even more openly and avowedly satiric than the "Epistles." In the "Epistles" the sketches, usually of abstracted or composite persons, were used structurally to illustrate the themes of the poems; in the "Imitations," they are more specific, although still fictive, and often embody within themselves the very object of attack.

This difference in the use of the sketch in the "Epistles" and in the "Imitations" points to another relationship between the two groups of poems. The ethical system as a whole is formal; but the degree of formality within it descends from the high, objective ceremoniousness of the "Essay on Man" to a less formal tone in the four epistles. In the "Imitations" the tone drops even lower— from that proper in a letter to one more fitting in conversation— and formality for the most part disappears. Since the first "Imitation" was written concurrently with the last part of "An Essay on Man," Pope doubtless looked upon its informal tone as a relief from the care required in the more philosophic work. According to his own statement, the "Imitations" could be (and were) dashed off as the mood or circumstances dictated:

But I must tell you it was not that idle poem which I meant my caution of, in my letter to your neighbour Cheselden. That was the work of two mornings, after my brain was heated by a fever.[1]

You may have seen my last piece of song, which has met with such a flood of favour that my ears need no more flattery for this twelve-month. However, it was a slight thing the work of two days, whereas that to Lord Bathurst was the work of two years by intervals.[2]

I've done another of Horace's Satires since I wrote to you last, and much in the same space of time as I did the former (tho' you don't be-lieve when I speak truth). The next time I'll compliment my own work better, and pretend it cost me more pains.[3]

Despite Pope's pose of deprecating the quality of the "Imita-tions," they were not the spontaneous, off-the-cuff, idle jottings that he pretended they were. As early as June 24, 1729, Elijah Fenton had reported to his fellow translator William Broome the following remark made to him by Pope: "I saw our friend Pope twice when I was at London. He inquired after your welfare, but said that you had dropped correspondence by not answering his last letter. The war is carried on against him furiously in pictures and libels; and I heard of nobody but Savage and Cleland who have yet drawn their pens in his defence. He told me that for the future he intended to write nothing but epistles in Horace's man-ner, in which I question not but he will succeed very well." [4]

Although the reference may be to the "Ethic Epistles," which also have Horatian models, rather than to the "Imitations" of Hor-ace's *Satires*, the Augustan concept of imitation would be the same: the "Imitations" are not lesser poems because they are imi-tative. Because "imitation" was not a derogatory term to the Au-gustans, (as the English neo-classical writers are called, since they were strongly influenced by writers in the reign of Caesar Augus-tus, just before the beginning of the Christian era), the "Imita-tions" would be as honorable a form of poetry as the "Epistles." Both genres had been practiced by Horace and had been sanc-tioned in the satires and verse epistles of Donne, Dryden, Old-ham, Roscommon, and other earlier English poets. Those poets, like Pope, tried to make the older traditions and forms speak to their own ages to enrich the present with the traditions of an older, respected civilization and, in a sense, to contribute to the past by continuing its culture into the present. One of Pope's favorite methods of "imitating" Horace is to take a theme or statement from the original, to create contemporary variations on it, and to illustrate it with portraits from the social or political scene. Pope also "imitated" by filling his lines with allusions from the earlier writers. This practice was not the mere copying of another poet; it was the presentation of the truth of a previous poet—one made alive and applicable to the present time by finding parallels and similarities between the ideas and modes of expression in the two ages.

One of the first poems Pope wrote was the "Ode on Solitude," an imitation of Horace. Throughout his life Pope continued to look upon Horace as his master, much in the manner that Dryden had been guided by Virgil. The presence of Horace is evident in varying ways as Pope's poetry matured. One hears his voice when Pope the critic expounds his conception of the poet and his work; one finds it also in Pope's ideas on culture, on the virtues of the contemplative rural life, on themes of patriotism, and on the need for urbane sophistication and moderation (the "golden mean"). In the "Imitations," it is the voice of Horace the satirist which one hear speaking in Pope's accents. Horace had described his *Satires* and *Epistles* as *saturae:* "small talks on almost any topic," or "conversations." In Pope's "Imitations," the Horatian conversational quality of friend speaking to friend predominates although the tone shifts from serious to gay, from cajolery to violent abuse, from raillery to formal oratory. Also in the spirit of Horace (*saturae*) is the rambling from one topic to another as Pope makes satiric thrusts at other issues than his major theme, or pauses to state a personal reflection or desire, or tells a story through narration or dialogue which in itself makes a satiric or moral comment.

Pope, in speaking through Horace, makes Horace his dramatic *persona.* He carefully creates and maintains this fictive personality as the speaker in the "Imitations." The speaker is not a man of violence; he is moderate, wise, urbane, poised; a judge, not a slanderer of morality, he is cultured, disciplined, and even-tempered. As such a man, he can indirectly, and thus ironically, note the discrepancies between appearances and reality; as an example of the moderate and virtuous man, he can judge others' actions by his own.[5]

I *"First Satire of the Second Book of Horace"*

Pope's first "Imitation" illustrates the quality of the genre: the random talk between friends on any subject that comes to mind. The friend is William Fortescue (1687–1749), a lawyer from whom Pope occasionally sought legal advice. According to Spence, the writing of the first "Imitation" was undertaken at the suggestion of Bolingbroke who, upon visiting Pope during an illness in January, 1733, and seeing a copy of Horace on the bedside table, proposed that Pope translate the first satire of the second book (*Sunt quibus in Satyra videar nimis acer et ultra*) because it fitted his situation. The original is Horace's apologia for writing satire, and Pope was then under attack for the "Timon" portrait in the "Epistle to Burlington." While Pope's version is also an apology for writing satire, it touches on several other topics that were to become favorites in the later "Imitations": George II's dislike for poetry; the lack of true art in contemporary art; irritation and anger at corruption in court circles; love of the contemplative life of solitude; and Lady Mary Wortley Montagu and Lord Hervey, along with lesser figures of vice and dullness.

Pope establishes and characterizes his *persona* throughout the poem:

> In me what Spots (for Spots I have) appear,
> Will prove at least the Medium must be clear.
> In this impartial Glass, my Muse intends
> Fair to expose myself, my Foes, my Friends.
>
> . . . .
>
> My Head and Heart thus flowing thro' my Quill,
> Verse-man or Prose-man, term me which you will,
> Papist or Protestant, or both between,
> Like good *Erasmus* in an honest Mean,
> In Moderation placing all my Glory,
> While Tories call me Whig, and Whigs a Tory.

. . . .

> Hear this, and tremble! you, who 'scape the Laws.
> Yes, while I live, no rich or noble knave
> Shall walk the World, in credit to his grave.
> TO VIRTUE ONLY AND HER FRIENDS, A FRIEND
> The World beside may murmur, or commend.
> (ll. 55–58, 63–68, 118–22)

The "Imitation" is more specific and concrete than the original. One feels that Pope must have had models for his characters; although they are fictional creatures of the imaginative process, Pope cites their names and particular misdeeds as he, in his letter of August 2, 1734, to Arbuthnot, insists that he must:

But General Satire in Times of General Vice has no force, & is no Punishment: People have ceas'd to be ashamed of it when so many are join'd with them; and tis only by hunting One or two from the Herd that any Examples can be made. If a man writ all his Life against the Collective Body of the Banditti, or against Lawyers, would it do the least Good, or lessen the Body? But if some are hung up, or pilloryed, it may prevent others. And in my low Station, with no other Power than this, I hope to deter, if not to reform.[6]

This practice of pillorying evildoers brought trouble to Pope's door. Lady Mary and Lord Hervey replied in March, 1733, with a vicious poem, entitled "Verses Addressed to the Imitator of Horace." Pope did not reply directly to the "Verses," but in the "Epistle to Arbuthnot," published in January, 1735, he answered Hervey in full and never ceased pricking Lady Mary in the rest of the "Imitations." Indirectly, Pope took notice of the "Verses" by publishing anonymously in 1733 "The Impertinent, Or a Visit to the Court," an adaptation of John Donne's "Fourth Satire," which castigates fops at court.

II *"Second Satire of the Second Book of Horace, Paraphrased"*

A letter to Swift dated April 2, 1733, states that Pope had just finished his next imitation, the "Second Satire of the Second Book of Horace, Paraphrased" (*Quae virtus et quanta, boni, sit vivere parvo*); the poem, however, was not published until July, 1734. The character of Horace's rough country fellow, Ofellus, is retained although unnamed by Pope and is based partly on Swift and partly on Hugh Bethel, one of the poet's lifelong friends. Through Bethel's conversation, the poem praises the virtues of the country life based upon the golden mean and excoriates the intemperance of courtiers, especially of Lady Mary and Lord Hervey. The *persona* of the poem then models himself along the lines of Bethel's character:

> Thus Bethel spoke, who always speaks his thought,
> And always thinks the very thing he ought:
> His equal mind I copy what I can,
> And as I love, would imitate the Man.   (ll. 129–32)

Pope chooses details from his own life which fit this characterization: "Tho' double-tax'd, how little have I lost?"/"My lands are sold, my Father's house is gone,"/"I'll hire another's [house], is not that my own?" Despite this adversity, the simple life is pleasant, and the man who lives it is his "own Master still."

III "Sober Advice from Horace"

The third poem of imitation, "Sober Advice from Horace," is based on the "Second Satire of the First Book of Horace" (*Ambubaiarum collegia, pharmacopolae*), a humorous treatment of the difficulties involved in committing adultery. Pope's version was published anonymously on December 21, 1734. Because the violence and near-pornographic quality of the poem aroused a storm of protest, Pope repudiated it by denying conjectures that he was its author, even to good friends like Caryll and the Earl of Oxford; but, by including the piece in his collected *Works* of 1738, he admitted its paternity. Pope's rendering loses the ironic humor implicit in the original; and the violence of his imagery constantly threatens to destroy the fabric from which the poem is woven.

IV "An Epistle to Dr. Arbuthnot"

On January 2, 1735, Pope published one of his best-known and finest poems, "An Epistle to Dr. Arbuthnot." The verse letter is classified as an imitation of Horace; but, not being based on any Horatian original it is rather a kind of free fantasia on Horatian themes that is cast into a conversational form after the manner of the Roman satirist. As Professor Brower comments, "The metaphor of the poem is simply Horace." [7] The poem, primarily a defense of Pope's career as a satirist, begins with a personal sketch of the poet's development but grows beyond this to a universal picture of the life of all successful writers who would reform through satire.

Pope wrote Swift that the "Epistle" had been written piecemeal over many years. The statement doubtless refers to various fragments of the poem, which had existed for some time independent of a context and were now put together into their epistolary form. When the poem was completed, Dr. Arbuthnot, long beloved by Pope, was incurably ill and near death. On the 17th of July, 1734, he wrote a "Last request" to Pope:

I must be so sincere as to own, that tho' I could not help valuing you for those Talents which the World prizes, yet they were not the Foundation of my Friendship: They were quite of another sort; nor shall I at present offend you by enumerating them: And I make it my Last Request, that you continue that noble *Disdain* and *Abhorrence* of Vice, which you seem naturally endu'd with, but still with a due regard to your own Safety; and study more to reform than chastise, tho' the one often cannot be effected without the other.[8]

Pope replied on September 3, 1734:

I have nothing to say more but that no Friend you have more warmly wishes your Recovery or your Ease, than I do. I took very kindly your Advice, concerning avoiding Ill-will from writing Satyr; & it has worked so much upon me (considering the *Time* & *State* you gave it in) that I determine to address to you one of my Epistles, written by piece-meal many years, & which I have now made haste to put together; wherein the Question is stated, what were, & are, my Motives of writing, the Objections to them, & my answers. It pleases me much to take this occasion of testifying (to the public at least, if not to Posterity) my Obligations & Friendship for, & from, you, for so many years: That is all that's in it; for Compliments are fulsome & go for nothing.[9]

Scholarship has traced these fragments which provide the flesh and sinews stretched over the Horatian skeleton of the poem. The most famous instance is the portrait of Addison—"Atticus" (ll. 151–214)—which, written as early as 1715, had been inspired by Addison's duplicity in the Ambrose Phillips-Pope controversy and the competitive Tickell translation of the *Iliad*. The lines were sent to Addison in 1716 and published, possibly without Pope's consent or knowledge, in the *St. James Journal* for December 15, 1722. Other short sections of the "Epistle" had also been either written or published earlier than 1734, when they were incorporated into the unified poem. Also in the background of the poem is Pope's continuing quarrel with Lady Mary Wortley Montagu and Lord Hervey. Lady Mary escapes with a few verbal bruises and lacerations, but the "Sporus" portrait for which Lord Hervey sat as model is without doubt the most damning character sketch in all English poetry (ll. 305–33).

But it would be unfair to both Pope and Lord Hervey to consider the portrait an accurate one. Professor Boyce's conclusions about the sketch are quite true:

The famous picture of Sporus, built up with damning phrases partly culled from previous pictures of Lord Hervey, is a different kind of example [from the idealization of a person]; for the man who fought a duel and begot eight children could not have been precisely and merely the creature Pope presented as Sporus. In order to create a shocking image of a special sort of vice Pope selected only certain aspects of a man who must have been in reality still more complex and curious than in the poem he seems. One is tempted to propose the neat generalization that in Pope's depictions the type tends to become more individual and the individual more typical. In the large I believe this is true. . . . Actually Pope has left us no pen-portrait of any known person that could properly be judged absolutely faithful, unbiased, and complete. Recollecting the liveliness and the penetrating observation of some of his sketches, one might for a moment regret this lack; one might wish that in place of the paintings of Swift that he threw away Pope had recorded in unforgettable words his full knowledge of his friend. But the wish is foolish. Pope was a great poet and a superb satirist; the great historian is something different.[10]

If the portrait (and that of "Atticus") is not a faithful portrayal of the actual man, the question arises as to why Pope distorted it.

The answer obviously resides in the function of the sktech within the poem. For one thing each sketch is an example of the particular vice under attack. The "Atticus" portrait comes at the conclusion of a section of the poem dealing with critics who had attacked Pope and his work from the very beginning: Gildon (l. 151), Dennis (l. 153), Theobald (l. 158), and Phillips (l. 179). In the "Sporus" sketch Pope presents a justification for his writing of satire. He has been arguing that he was by nature impelled to write and that attacks upon him forced him to defend himself; but, in turning to satire, he restricted his Muse to attacking vicious gossips and to exalting virtue; therefore, his satire has not feared to reveal vice in high places nor has it been aggressive. Sporus is the classic example of the vicious gossip, and the sketch concludes the section of the poem which defends the practice of attacking such people.

The character sketches also serve as a structural device within the poem. They help, by contrast, to define the character of the *persona* as the modest man. Highly successful in his writing, he is subject to all manner of jealous attack; yet, despite all this, he remains a friend to virtue and a foe of vice. Moreover, the sketches, through their imagery, allow Pope to set into motion ever-widening circles of meaning for the whole poem. The "Atticus" sketch, when compared to that of "Sporus," is more subtle and its technique more formal. Antithesis is the dominant literary device used for Atticus, and this rhetorical figure, along with the use of the subjunctive mood, mirrors Addison's hesitancy in pronouncing critical judgment on the work of others. The antithesis also echoes Addison's deliberately calculated destruction of rival writers by phrasing his comments with such objectivity that they damned while they seemed to praise. The carefully balanced antitheses also suggest the antithetical nature of his criticism, a quality which made Addison a lamentable, negative force rather than a positive one in letters and criticism

The "Sporus" portrait, however, is anything but subtle. The imagery constantly echoes *Paradise Lost*, Sporus finally cringing as an effeminate, degenerate Satan; and the vice of gossip which he illustrates is grounded in the "Father of Lies" himself. The evil of Sporus is associated with negation: he is described as "impotence," an "Amphibious thing," "one vile Antithesis," the possessor of a "Pride that licks the Dust." The speaker's disgust at this evil lack of direction is intensified by associating the qualities of Sporus with insects, animals, and filth: "Ass," "butterfly," "stinks and stings," a toothless "spaniel," "toad," "venom," and "reptile."

This affirmation of an active force as good and a negative one as bad is one of Pope's most firmly held beliefs. It had been the major theme or a closely related one in every significant poem he had written thus far in his career, and almost every character sketch in his poems is based upon this active-good, negative-bad polarity. "Sporus" is Pope's portrait of the greatest evil he knew—that of a negation born of contraries, a hermaphroditism which by its very nature must be sterile.

After the virulence of the "Sporus" portrayal, Pope's speaker, in contrast, can quietly but all the more effectively turn to his own life and unaggressive conduct. This he does by idealizing the life of his parents who were content with humble blessings, a theme which provides a transition to the conclusion of the "Epistle": the benediction asking that God bestow these same blessings on Arbuthnot.

V *Imitations of John Donne*

In 1735, the same year that the "Epistle to Arbuthnot" was published, Pope also issued the second volume of his collected *Works,* which contained two imitations of Donne: "The Second Satire of Dr. John Donne," and the "Fourth Satire of Dr. John Donne." Pope claims in the "Advertisement" to the "Imitations of Horace" that he "versified" Donne's satires "at the Desire of the Earl of *Oxford* while he was Lord treasurer, and of the Duke of *Shrewsbury.*" This statement would date the original versions between 1711 and 1714, a period of poetic apprenticeship during which Pope was engaged in modernizing, then in imitating, Chaucer. There is no reason to doubt the early date for the Donne imitations; but, because of references in the poems to contemporary events, Pope undoubtedly revised them (at least the two which are extant) sometime after 1730 and brought their tone into line with the "Imitations of Horace." "The Second Satire of Dr. John Donne" is not equal to the Horatian imitations, possibly because less original work was involved, translation from another language not being necessary.

The "Fourth Satire," revised after its anonymous publication in 1733, is of interest because it shows Pope's growing involvement in politics. In the adaptation Donne's fop becomes a typical courtier, and his gossip includes comments on the political issues which were paramount in 1734, an election year. The courtier's remarks, critical of Walpole's government, reveal Pope's sympathies with the opposition. After the elections of 1734, the new Parliament included some of Pope's new friends in the opposition, and until the next governmental crisis of 1737 his poetry is relatively nonpolitical in nature.

It is most likely that Lord Cobham (to whom the first "Ethic Epistle" had been addressed) introduced Pope to George Lyttleton,[11] Lord Polwarth,[12] and Sir William Wyndham,[13] all three being younger members of the opposition party. The opposition never functioned effectively because of a deep split in its ranks. It had been organized by William Pulteney[14] and Bolingbroke, but the aims of the two men differed greatly: Pulteney and Lord Carteret[15] had become the leaders of the faction containing disaffected Whigs who opposed Walpole for reasons of personal power and selfish gain; Bolingbroke led the other group which was composed largely of idealistic young men who desired genuine governmental reform. For the most part, these young men were Tories; but some young Whigs were among them. Pope's sympathies were with the group of young idealists, as a letter to Swift on December 30, 1736, indicates:

You ask me if I have got any supply of new Friends to make up for those that are gone? I think that impossible, for not our friends only, but so much of our selves is gone by the mere flux and course of years, that were the same Friends to be restored to us, we could not be restored to our selves, to enjoy them. . . . I have acquired, without my seeking, a few chance-acquaintance, of young men, who look rather to the past age than the present, and therefore the future may have some hopes of them. If I love them, it is because they honour some of those whom I, and the world, have lost, or are losing. Two or three of them have distinguish'd themselves in Parliament, and you will own in a very uncommon manner, when I tell you it is by their asserting of Independency, and contempt of Corruption. One or two are link'd to me by their love of the same studies and the same authors: but I will own to you, my moral capacity has got so much the better of my poetical, that I have few acquaintance on the latter score, and none without a casting weight on the former.[16]

Owing to a split, the opposition party lost the elections of 1734, and any future effectiveness of the group was impaired to such a degree that Bolingbroke, disheartened, retired to France in 1735. The "Horatian Imitations" often make reference to these intra-party troubles, and the basic cause of the split—Tory idealism and Whig practicality—can be seen everywhere in the "Imitations." It is embodied in the poems in terms of the traditional association of Toryism with the country and Whiggism with the city elements of the electorate. Furthermore, two contrasting views are used in the poems as two opposing sets of values, which correspond to Horace's contrast of the retired, country life with its simple rule of moderation to the city-court life with its luxury, corruption, and decadence. The country life, furthermore, functions as a metaphor in the "Imitations." It implies a oneness with nature, stressed earlier in "Windsor Forest," in the "Essay on Man," and in the "Ethic Epistles"; it represents the ideal life founded on the values lacking in a merchant, moneyed, urban society.

These opposing sets of values are emphasized more strongly in those "Imitations of Horace" which were published after the 1734 elections. Evidently Pope's political interests were whetted by his new friends in the opposition, and his political views loomed larger as part of his total view of the disintegration of society. From 1734 to 1737 he published no imitation of Horace; he was busy seeing through the press his collected *Works*, the "Epistle to Dr. Arbuthnot," and the second "Ethic Epistle: On the Characters of Women," all of which came out in 1735. The following year he remained silent. In 1737, however, he published three more imitations: "The First Ode of the Fourth Book of Horace: to Venus," in March; "The Second Epistle of the Second Book of Horace," in April; and "The First Epistle of the Second Book of Horace," in May.

This resurgence of writing was probably inspired by another political crisis which promised to unseat Walpole. The Prince of Wales, who was a personal friend of Pope and had visited him at Twickenham, was not only an enemy of Walpole but hostile to his

father, King George II.[17] During the year, the prince aligned himself openly with the opposition and was ready to do battle with
his father and the prime minister. The king had kept his son on a
small allowance, and finally in anger and desperation the prince
asked Parliament to debate his finances publicly. Because of the
divisive nature of the opposition, Walpole won the vote by a small
majority. Also, Spanish raids on English shipping in 1737–38, acts
which Walpole refused to meet with force, had further reduced
the minister's popularity. It was an opportune moment for the
opposition under the leadership of the Prince of Wales to defeat
Walpole and to assume control of the government. At this juncture of events, Pope in May published "One Thousand Seven
Hundred and Thirty Eight. Dialogue II."

VI *"Horace His Ode to Venus"*

The first of the three imitations published in 1737 was "Horace
His Ode to Venus" (*Inter missa Venus diu*). There is no political
comment in the ode. Undoubtedly Pope found Horace's ode
slightly relevant in an amusing way to his own personal situation:
he is now a "sober fifty" (actually forty-nine) and "For me, the
vernal Garlands bloom no more" (1. 32); therefore, he prays that
Venus will "direct her Doves" to the house of William Murray,[18]
one of the poet's new friends in the opposition party.

VII *"Second Epistle of the Second Book of Horace"*

The second of the three poems, the "Second Epistle of the Second Book of Horace" (*Flore, bono claroque fidelis amice Neroni*),
has, however, an undertone which indirectly criticizes the court
and the city as unproductive of art (poetry). The "Epistle" is reminiscent of that to Arbuthnot, particularly in its details and illustrations drawn from Pope's personal tribulations in trying to survive literary ambition. The verse letter is addressed to a "Dear
Col'nel," who "loves a Verse"; but beyond Pope's statement that
he was a friend of Lord Cobham, he still remains unidentified. A
couplet obliquely implies that the Colonel helped make the laws,
so perhaps he was a member of Parliament: "You said the same;
and are you discontent/With Laws, to which you gave your own
assent?" (ll. 29–30).

The political comments, for the most part, are indirect and enter the poem as observations on the restrictive laws that were obstacles to Pope's training as a poet:

> And certain Laws, by Suff'rers thought unjust,
> Deny'd all Posts of Profit or of Trust:
> Hopes after Hopes of pious Papists fail'd,
> While mighty WILLIAM's thundring Arm prevail'd.
> For Right Hereditary tax'd and fin'd,
> He stuck to Poverty with Peace of Mind;
> And me, the Muses help'd to undergo it;
> Convict a Papist He, and I a Poet.
> But (thanks to *Homer*) since I live and thrive,
> Indebted to no Prince or Peer alive,
> Sure I should want the Care of ten *Monroes*,
> If I would scribble, rather than repose.   (ll. 58–71)

After establishing his character as self-made and honest, the poet-speaker passes on to other obstacles to poetic fame, obstacles which are in nature or society, not in the law. One of these is time itself, and he notes in memorable lines echoing Milton the depredations that "the subtle thief of youth" has made:

> Years foll'wing Years, steal something ev'ry day,
> At last they steal us from ourselves away;
> In one our Frolicks, one Amusements end,
> In one a Mistress drops, in one a Friend:
> This subtle Thief of Life, this paltry Time,
> What will it leave me, if it snatch my Rhime?
> If ev'ry Wheel of that unweary'd Mill
> That turn'd ten thousand Verses, now stands still.
> (ll. 72–79)

But, even if a poet withstands time and the demands of his audience, the moral degradation of the day works against poetry which is a serious art concerned with the refinement of language (ll. 153–79) and "flows from Art, not Chance" (l. 178). This art cannot be created amid the distractions and evils of London, but

> Soon as I enter at my Country door,
> My Mind resumes the thread it dropt before;
> Thoughts, which at Hyde-Park-Corner I forgot,

> Meet and rejoin me, in the pensive Grott.
> There all alone, and Compliments apart,
> I ask the sober questions of my Heart.   (ll. 206–11)

If in meditation one asks and answers the "questions of his Heart," the inequities and corruptions rampant in society and government will become evident, and these are recounted with specific names of offenders and of laws which maintain the abuses. After castigating these evils the speaker returns to the praise of the golden mean, on which he has based his life. The "Epistle" then closes with an admonition to the Colonel to follow the poet-speaker's moderate view of life:

> Learn to live well, or fairly make your Will;
> You've play'd, and lov'd, and eat, and drank your fill:
> Walk sober off; before a sprightlier Age
> Comes titt'ring on, and shoves you from the stage:
> Leave such a trifle with more grace and ease,
> Whom Folly pleases, and whose Follies please.   (ll. 322–27)

The closing passage, however, has a pessimistic quality which belies the stated theme of happiness achieved through moderation. The specter of old age haunts the poem, and it is too somber and real to be treated in the amusing manner of Horace. But aside from his "black Fear of Death, that saddens all" the speaker seems to realize that satire and art are passing from the scene and that a "sprightlier Age" has come "titt'ring on"—an age in which "Folly" reigns and little can be done to reform it. The optimism expressed in "An Essay on Man" and in the "Ethic Epistles" is lacking in this imitation of Horace; the tone is closer to that of the "Dunciad" in which darkness eclipses the light of hope. The poem seems to prefigure that final work, which sees the actual world as a nightmare of distortion and negation.

VIII   *"First Epistle of the Second Book of Horace: to Augustus"*

The third imitation published in 1737 is one of Pope's masterpieces: "The First Epistle of the Second Book of Horace" (*Cum tot sustineas et tanta negotia, solus*). It is modeled on Horace's epistle to Caesar Augustus who, according to Suetonius, requested

Horace to address a work to him. Horace pays tribute to the power and the glory of the emperor; he praises Augustus for restoring order and giving a sense of tradition and continuity to Roman life, for patronizing art and artists, and for recognizing their necessity and contribution to the vital life of the nation. When Pope adapts these compliments to George Augustus II of England, his consummate irony turns praise to mockery and admiration to disgust. Pope's imitation is filtered through the Horatian original, and Horace and his poem become the structural metaphor of Pope's imitation.

To help create this ironic tone, the speaker in Pope's imitation is naïve and unsophisticated. He addresses George Augustus with reverence and humility, casting his speech in the appropriate heroic style:

> While You, great Patron of Mankind, sustain
> The balanc'd World, and open all the Main;
> Your Country, chief, in Arms abroad defend,
> At home, with Morals, Arts, and Laws amend;
> How shall the Muse, from such a Monarch, steal
> An hour, and not defraud the Publick Weal?
>
> . . . .
>
> To Thee, the World its present homage pays,
> The Harvest early, but mature the Praise:
> Great Friend of LIBERTY! in *Kings* a Name
> Above all Greek, above all Roman Fame:
> Whose Word is Truth, as sacred and rever'd,
> As Heav'n's own Oracles from Altars heard.
> Wonder of Kings! like whom, to mortal eyes
> None e'er has risen, and none e'er shall rise.   (ll. 1–6, 23–30)

The application of the heroic style to an unheroic figure like George, who was regarded by his people as pusillanimous and parsimonious, produces a mockery of the highest order. The opening and closing lines of the poem (1–30, 390–403) are mock panegyric, but the main body of the "Epistle" is Pope's evaluation of life and society under George II. In this section the irony subsides, although the literary taste, false moral values, and standards of life engendered by the age are under attack. Pope follows Horace more closely here than in the parts of the poem which dispraise George.

Caesar Augustus had recognized the value of the poet and his work in the functioning of the Roman state and civilization; George Augustus recognizes no such thing. The main section of the poem, then, justifies the poet and poetry in an age in which the artist is no longer granted dignity and standing in the life of the nation. George's age grudgingly paid lip service to older writers but could see no value in contemporary ones. Pope attacks this veneration of antiquity for the sake of antiquity; and, after citing the strengths and weaknesses of several Renaissance, Jacobean, and Restoration poets, he concludes:

> Had ancient Times conspir'd to dis-allow
> What then was new, what had been ancient now?
> Or what remain'd, so worthy to be read
> By learned Criticks, of the mighty Dead?   (ll. 135–38)

Since the "ancients" were "moderns" in their own day, modern poets should be valued before they become ancient, because they can be "of some weight/And (tho' no Soldier) useful to the State" (ll. 202–3). Poetry teaches moral virtue, as the writings of Addison illustrate:

> And in our own (excuse some Courtly stains)
> No whiter page than Addison remains.
> He from the taste obscene reclaims our Youth,
> And sets the Passions on the side of Truth;
> Forms the soft bosom with the gentlest art,
> And pours each human Virtue in the heart.   (ll. 215–20)

Poetry also has the power to preserve human rights, as the work of Swift proves:

> Let Ireland tell, how Wit upheld her cause,
> Her Trade supported, and supply'd her Laws;
> And leave on Swift this grateful verse ingrav'd,
> The Rights a Court attack'd, a Poet sav'd.
> Behold the hand that wrought a Nation's cure,
> Stretch'd to relieve the Idiot and the Poor,
> Proud Vice to brand, or injur'd Worth adorn,
> And stretch the Ray to Ages yet unborn.   (ll. 221–28)

Poetry further provides pleasure for leisure hours; and, when license threatens the land, it defends the nation's virtue: "Hence Satire rose, that just the medium hit,/And heals with Morals what it hurts with Wit" (ll. 261–62).

The one form of contemporary literary art which does not come up to these standards is the drama. It has become the victim of "the many-headed Monster of the Pit"—a vulgar taste, which now universally demands farce:

> What dear delight to Britons Farce affords!
> Ever the taste of Mobs, but now of Lords;
> (Taste, that eternal wanderer, which flies
> From heads to ears, and now from ears to eyes.)
> (ll. 310–13)

But taste is not the only corrupter of poets; in seeking fame and recognition, poets prostitute themselves:

> But most, when straining with too weak a wing,
> We needs will write Epistles to the King;
> And from the moment we oblige the town,
> Expect a Place, or Pension from the Crown;
> Or dubb'd Historians by express command,
> T'enroll your triumphs o'er the seas and land;
> Be call'd to Court, to plan some work divine,
> As once for Louis, Boileau and Racine.   (ll. 368–75)

At this point, irony enters the poem again, as the naïve speaker comments that another value of poetry is to praise great monarchs and that only the greatest of poets would be fit to sing the virtues of George Augustus. The context would define such a poet as the greatest prostitute in the land.

The "Epistle to Augustus" is one of Pope's most subtle poems. He dared considerable risk of prosecution in writing the satire, and part of the subtlety of the poem doubtless results from this fact. But Pope did not want readers (often literal in the eighteenth century) to misunderstand his mockery. The closing lines of the poem remove all doubt, even that of the most obtuse reader:

> But Verse alas! your Majesty disdains;
> And I'm not us'd to Panegyric strains:
> The Zeal of Fools offends at any time,
> But most of all, the Zeal of Fools in ryme.
> Besides, a fate attends on all I write,
> That when I aim at praise, they say I bite.
> A vile Encomium doubly ridicules;
> There's nothing blackens like the ink of fools;
> If true, a woful likeness, and if lyes,
> 'Praise undeserv'd is scandal in disguise.'   (ll. 404–13)

Although the burden of the poem is a defense of poetry in Pope's day, there is no strong feeling that the prestige of poetry will rise. The nostalgia and yearning for the golden days of the Stuarts, when a poet was not without honor, overshadow the hope implicit in the defense of Hanoverian poetry. Moreover, since the poem centers its attack on George and his court as being responsible for the degraded taste of the age, there is no soil in which hope can be planted.

IX *"Sixth Epistle of the First Book of Horace"; "Sixth Satire of the Second Book of Horace"; "First Epistle of the First Book of Horace"; and "Seventh Epistle of the First Book of Horace"*

The following year Pope again published three more Horatian imitations: "The Sixth Epistle of the First Book of Horace" (January, 1738); "The Sixth Satire of the Second Book of Horace" (March); and "The First Epistle of the First Book of Horace" (March). The first of these, "The Sixth Epistle of the First Book" (*Nil admirari, prope res est una, Numici*), was addressed to William Murray, his young friend in the opposition. The satire is direct, possessing none of the ironic finesse and subtlety of the "Epistle to Augustus." Pope takes the opening lines from Horace as a moral text for his version: " 'Not to Admire, is all the Art I know,/'To make men happy, and to keep them so' " (ll. 1–2).

The present evil day (Murray's and Pope's) with its false standards of value offers the man of ambition and worth all the happiness that the power, wealth, and glory of the world can bring—if he will only bow his knee to that world as his master. But these are seductions; and true happiness, the speaker points out, lies in virtue, the golden mean of moderation. The poem has a simple but admirable construction; but, despite its clarity, its bald sententiousness is too weighty for the examples to make it interesting. The element of the "sermon" intrudes upon the element of "conversation"; as a result, the epistle lacks the sparkle which so often gleams in the other "Imitations."

"The Sixth Satire of the Second Book" (*Hoc erat in botis; modus agri non ita magnus*) was written by Swift in 1714 and published in the third volume of the Pope-Swift *Miscellanies* (1728). Although there is room for doubt, it seems quite likely that Pope added two sections (lines 9–28 and 133–221) to the poem when he reissued it at this date. The "Satire" is addressed to Robert Harley, the Earl of Oxford, who had been the Tory leader. The poem amusingly recounts the difficulties Swift experienced in serving the government of Harley, the demands made on his time by people begging him to intercede for them, and his longing for the quiet life of retreat in the country where moderation, simplicity, and true friendship dwell. The poem concludes with a "moral" in the form of the fable of the town and the country mice who visit each other.

"The First Epistle of the First Book" (*Prima dicte mihi summa dicende Camena!*) is an imitation of Horace's epistle to his friend and patron, Gaius Cilnius Maecenas, an aristocratic adviser to Caesar Augustus. As Horace had dedicated his "First Book of Epistles" to Maecenas by addressing him in the opening lines of the poem, so Pope pays tribute to his Maecenas, Bolingbroke,[19] whose shadow lengthens across the Horatian "Imitations" from the first one, which was written at Bolingbroke's suggestion, to the final "Dialogue II" with its tribute "Why rail they then, if but a Wreath of Mine/Oh All-accomplish'd St. John! deck thy Shrine?" (l. 138–39).

The original epistle of Horace to Maecenas avowed Horace's intention to study philosophy and to discontinue his writing. The *persona* of Pope's imitation is an older, wiser man of the world who, in reviewing his life with its changing courses and aims, comes to the final truth that "The first Wisdom [of man is] to be Fool no more" (l. 66). Therefore, he will study philosophy "To stop thy foolish views, thy long desires,/And ease thy heart of all that it admires" (ll. 75–76). The truth which comes from this study will close the ears of the speaker to the voice of the city crying " 'Get Mony, Mony still' "; it will teach him to avoid the court with its corruption; and it will protect him from the false values of society, whose individual members share only one thing in common—the "Lust of Gold." The one person who is the exception and atonement for these satirized follies is Bolingbroke, and the poem ends with an apostrophe to him containing higher praise than Pope saw fit to offer any other friend in all his poetry:

> Is this my Guide, Philosopher, and Friend?
> This, he who loves me, and who ought to mend?
> Who ought to make me (what he can, or none,)
> That Man divine whom Wisdom calls her own,
> Great without Title, without Fortune bless'd,
> Rich ev'n when plunder'd, honour'd while oppress'd,
> Lov'd without youth, and follow'd without power,
> At home tho' exiled, free, tho' in the Tower.
> In short, that reas'ning, high, immortal Thing,
> Just less than Jove, and much above a King,
> Nay half in Heav'n—except (what's mighty odd)
> A Fit of Vapours clouds this Demi-god.   (ll. 177–88)

Horace had also addressed his seventh "Epistle" (*Quinque dies tibi pollicitus me rure futurum*) to Maecenas. In the collected *Works* of 1739, Pope published his imitation of it "in the Manner of Dr. Swift." A few references in the text suggest that the imitation was written in 1737 and that it also was addressed to Bolingbroke although St. John's name is not specifically mentioned. The verse letter contains only eighty-four lines and urges the simple, moderate life which bestows honesty and independence upon those who follow it.

The specific citing of actual persons by name and the allusive nature of the "Imitations" inevitably invited attack on Pope by his old adversaries and by new ones paid by Walpole's government to silence the poet. Pope's outspoken praise of Bolingbroke, the arch-enemy of the government, in the "First Epistle of the First Book" (March, 1738), brought the storm to its climactic fury in April, when scurrilous attacks against Pope were published. A year later Pope wrote Swift describing the past incident, and his comments in the letter show that he felt the need to defend the satirical nature of the "Imitations": "You compliment me in vain upon retaining my Poetical Spirit. I am sinking fast into prose; & if I ever write more, it ought, (at these years, & in these Times) to be something, the Matter of which will give value to the Work, not merely the Manner. Since my *Protest, (for so I call the Dialogue of* 1738) *I have written but ten lines, which I will send you. They are an Insertion for the next New Edition of the Dunciad. . . ."* [20]

X "*Epilogue to the Satires, Dialogue I and Dialogue II*"

Pope's next imitation, "One Thousand Seven Hundred and Thirty Eight," published May 16, 1738, was primarily a defense of himself and his satire. But it also seems to have been part of a new plan: to issue a series of poems, each of which would be a "Dialogue Something like Horace" dwelling on the state of affairs in England during the year named in the title. That Pope had some such scheme in mind is suggested by an unpublished fragmentary dialogue, "One Thousand Seven Hundred and Forty," first published by Warburton in the 1751 edition of the poet's works. The many ellipses and the inflammatory nature of the fragment indicate that Pope feared prosecution if the poem were published. It was, perhaps, partly a fear of prosecution that caused Pope to abandon his scheme to issue a poem for each year. Instead he published a second dialogue, "One Thousand Seven Hundred and Thirty Eight" on July 18, 1738, just two months after the first one. It has been suggested by the editors of the Twickenham Edition that lines one to three and 248–49 of "Dialogue II" indicate that Pope feared that government censorship was imminent, and that he therefore had to publish his dialogue as soon as possible. The final couplet of "Dialogue II" offers an alternate explanation for the change in plans: "*Fr.* Alas! alas! pray end what you began,/ And write next winter more Essays on Man" (ll. 254–55). Perhaps Pope, now under the influence of Warburton, was turning his mind once more to that ethical system which he had abandoned some four years earlier. Whatever his reasons, Pope conceived of the two "Dialogues" as the last of the Horatian imitations; and he combined them in the 1740 edition of his works under one title, "Epilogue to the Satires."

"Dialogue I" is a conversation (seemingly more public than private) between *Pope* and an anonymous friend, *Fr.*, a politic and temporizing creature, His talk possesses the "sly, polite, insinuating stile" of Horace in his role of "artful Manager" (ll. 19–21). Against this cynic, with his realistic advice to accept the world as it is, is opposed the other speaker, *Pope*, who is a blunt, plain-speaking man committed to an uncompromising moral view. The technique of the poem is reminiscent of "To Bathurst," in which the protagonist and the antagonist duel verbally until agreement is reached in a compromise or reconciliation of the opposing views. The conclusions of the two poems, however, differ in that "Dialogue I" ends in no reconciliation. The tone of *Pope* drowns out that of *Fr.* to the same degree that his ironic argument reveals the puerility of *Fr.'s* position. *P.* accepts *Fr.'s* argument that "Virtue is an empty boast," and goes on to defend the "Dignity of Vice" (ll. 113–14). In so doing, the irony of the passage proves the falsity of the realist who would accept the world as it is. In such a world, the lowest imitate the vices of the highest, and the highest are the worst; vice has no dignity, and virtue is an empty boast; there are no values and no distinctions possible in *Fr.'s* world.

P. pursues his inverted argument to its ultimate conclusion. Virtue, unlike vice, is without class distinction:

> Virtue may chuse the high or low Degree,
> 'Tis just alike to Virtue, and to me;
> Dwell in a Monk, or light upon a King,
> She's still the same, belov'd, contented thing.   (ll. 137–40)

In the world of the realist, however, vice is class-conscious; her dignity resides in her dwelling with the great of the land. She reigns over the society which the realist wants *P.* to accept as it is. The moral tone of *P.* loses its ironic edge as he draws a bitter and terrifying picture of the world as it really is, a hell where vice is virtue, innocence is shame, and villainy is sacred:

> *Vice* is undone, if she forgets her Birth,
> And stoops from Angels to the Dregs of Earth:
> But 'tis the *Fall* degrades her to a Whore;
> Let Greatness own her, and she's mean no more:
> Her Birth, her Beauty, Crowds and Courts confess,
> Chaste Matrons praise her, and grave Bishops bless:

In golden Chains the willing World she draws,
And hers the Gospel is, and hers the Laws:
Mounts the Tribunal, lifts her scarlet head,
And sees pale Virtue carted in her stead!
Lo! at the Wheels of her Triumphal Car,
Old *England's* Genius, rough with many a Scar,
Dragg'd in the Dust! his Arms hang idly round,
His Flag inverted trails along the ground!
Our Youth, all liv'ry'd o'er with foreign Gold,
Before her dance; behind her crawl the Old!
See thronging Millions to the Pagod run,
And offer Country, Parent, Wife, or Son!
Hear her black Trumpet thro' the Land Proclaim,
That 'Not to be corrupted is the Shame.'
In Soldier, Churchman, Patriot, Man in Pow'r,
'Tis Av'rice all, Ambition is no more!
See, all our Nobles begging to be Slaves!
See, all our Fools aspiring to be Knaves!
The Wit of Cheats, the Courage of a Whore,
Are what ten thousand envy and adore.
All, all look up, with reverential Awe,
On Crimes that scape, or triumph o'er the Law:
While Truth, Worth, Wisdom, daily they decry—
'Nothing is Sacred now but Villany.'   (ll. 141–70)

This passage echoes the description of the fall of the evil angels in Book II of *Paradise Lost*, possibly tracing a parallel between Vice and Belial to whom no special altar smoked because he was worshiped not by any particular group but by all evil men. Pope's imagery indicates his belief in the apotheosis of Vice by his age, an imagery which culminates in the final line with a statement of the new creed of this worship. Supporting this religious imagery are other images, scattered throughout both "Dialogues," which emphasize the subhuman qualities of a mankind which worships vice. Animal-man comparisons (seen in a milder form in the "Epistle to Dr. Arbuthnot") and nauseous excremental details (to be surpassed only in the "Dunciad") abound in the "Dialogues." There can be no doubt of his deep disgust and his abhorrence of that "pernicious race of little odious vermin" called man. The bitterness of this indictment of the moral negativism in human nature and society is equaled only in the forth book of the "Dun-

ciad" in which he describes the nightmare of a world lost in moral
darkness.

After this vision of the moral degradation of England in 1738, a
single couplet concludes but does not resolve the argument: "Yet
may this Verse (if such a Verse remain)/Show there was one who
held it in disdain" (ll. 171–72). It does not resolve the debate because the speaker neither comes to terms with nor attempts to
reform the corrupt society depicted; instead, he withdraws from
this real world, defended by *Fr.*, into that of his own moral isolation, into a world which has moral values for himself but one
which the context of the poem has defined as unreal. This withdrawal is not the usual Horatian pose of retreat to the countryside, where one might pursue simple pleasures and enjoy rejuve-
nation through meditation. There is no hope or optimism in this
retirement; satire is left behind because the world will not be re-
formed; only moral disgust at the world remains; and the speaker,
devoid of hope, turns his back upon it.

"Dialogue II" is debated by the same opponents, *P.* and *Fr.*;
but the dramatic situation of the poem is considerably different. *P.*
is a hunter looking for game of the species Vice; *Fr.* is the opponent who knows more about the game laws than does the hunter.
The game laws are not only government restrictions but also social mores which protect the vicious from the weapon of satire:

> *P.*   I fain wou'd please you, if I knew with what:
> Tell me, which Knave is lawful Game, which not?
> Must great Offenders, once escap'd the Crown,
> Like Royal Harts, be never more run down?
> Admit your Law to spare the Knight requires;
> As Beasts of Nature may we hunt the Squires?
> Suppose I censure—you know what I mean—
> To save a Bishop, may I name a Dean?
> *Fr.*   A dean, Sir? no: his Fortune is not made,
> You hurt a man that's rising in the Trade.
> *P.*   If not the Tradesman who set up today,
> Much less the 'Prentice who tomorrow may.
> Down, down, proud Satire! tho' a Realm be spoil'd,
> Arraign no mightier Thief than wretched *Wild*,
> Or if a Court or Country's made a Job,
> Go drench a Pick-pocket, and join the Mob.   (ll. 26–41)

P. eventually learns from the cynical casuist *Fr.* that there is no prey that the satirist may hunt. As an honest, incorruptible citizen, *P.* objects strenuously to a relativism that refuses to distinguish between Good and Bad, Virtue and Vice:

> Ask you what Provocation I have had?
> The strong Antipathy of Good to Bad.
> When Truth or Virtue an Affront endures,
> Th' Affront is mine, my Friend, and should be yours.
> Mine, as a Foe profess'd to false Pretence,
> Who think a Coxcomb's Honour like his Sense;
> Mine, as a Friend to ev'ry worthy mind;
> And mine as Man, who feel for all mankind.   (ll. 197–204)

The whole of "Dialogue II" is devoted to the defense of satire as the servant of Good and as the scourge of Bad. But the social evils, which the poem enumerates, and the forces ranged against satire are considerably stronger than "the last Pen for Freedom [drawn]!/When Truth stands trembling on the edge of Law" (ll. 248–9). *P.*'s tone becomes more shrill as the debate turns into public harangue, and *P.* again withdraws from the world into moral isolation:

> *Fr.*   You're strangely proud.   *P.*   So proud, I am no Slave:
> So impudent, I own myself no Knave:
> So odd, my Country's ruin makes me grave.
> Yes, I am proud; I must be proud to see
> Men not afraid of God, afraid of me.   (ll. 205–9)

But even the noble realm of the mind is not completely free from the ignoble demands of the corrupt, real world. The spokesman of that cynical world, *Fr.*, has the final word as he exhorts *P.* to go back to painting rosy, optimistic pictures of man in harmony with the world: "Alas! alas! pray end what you began,/And write next winter more *Essays on Man*" (ll. 254–55).

The hopelessness evident in this couplet, seen in the context of the whole poem, must have resulted from more than mere fear of government censorship. It cannot be adequately explained by Pope's dejection at the failure of the Tories to gain control of the government. Pope's interest in politics was never partisan; rather, he was concerned about the immoral effects on mankind of bad government, whether Tory or Whig. Nor can the tone of hopelessness be accounted for by Warburton's tepid explanation that Pope was tired of imitating Horace. Pope's own note appended to these lines expresses a profound world-weariness and the satirist's sense of frustration at trying to change a way of life which had triumphed and was being worshiped in his day:

This was the last poem of the kind printed by our author, with a resolution to publish no more; but to enter thus, in the most plain and solemn manner he could, a sort of PROTEST against that insuperable corruption and depravity of manners, which he had been so unhappy as to live to see. Could he have hoped to have amended any, he had continued those attacks; but bad men were grown so shameless and so powerful, that Ridicule was become as unsafe as it was ineffectual. The Poem raised him, as he knew it would, some enemies; but he had reason to be satisfied with the approbation of good men, and the testimony of his own conscience.[21]

The futility of writing satire to change a stiff-necked generation no doubt caused Pope to write finis to the "Horatian Imitations," which as a group he considered his body of satire, and to give to the two dialogues of 1738 the title, "Epilogue to the Satires." The pessimistic view of man which characterizes these two poems is retained in Pope's last work, "The Dunciad," which is a prophecy of what this world will become. The fact that this outlook dominates the later "Imitations" and inspires the final version of the "Dunciad" indicates that the poet's earlier vision of man working in harmony with nature—as seen in "Windsor Forest," "Messiah," "An Essay on Man," and the "Ethic Epistles"—has given way to a darker view of human nature as unregenerate and as in perpetual discord with the world.

CHAPTER 5

The Twilight of the Gods

I *"The Dunciad"*

AFTER Pope had completed the "Imitations of Horace," his creative impulses lay dormant for two years—until awakened through his meeting with the Reverend Warburton. The result was the publication in March, 1742, of the fourth book of the "Dunciad—The New Dunciad: As it was Found in the Year 1741." This new work is the fulfillment of the prophecies uttered in the concluding lines of the two poems which comprised the "Epilogue to the Satires." Pope was to revise "The Dunciad" again, but this fourth book embodied his final comment on the state of mid-eighteenth-century civilization and describes his vision of the age to come.

Because Pope saw fit at the end of his life to return a fourth time to a poem which he had conceived as early as 1726, it seems reasonable to assume that he considered it one of his major works. During Swift's visit to Pope in March, 1726, the two friends sorted through the old Martinus Scriblerus papers. One of the fragments saved from the fire was an early version of the "Dunciad." Professor Sherburn has suggested that this first version had been occasioned by the choice of Elkanah Settle as the "City Poet" for 1719.[1] When Swift again visited Pope in April of the following year (1727), he wrote a poem describing Pope at work on the "Dunciad."[2] This early version of Pope's poem was published May 18, 1728, as "The Dunciad." Although Pope had published the poem anonymously, his authorship was an open secret.

The success of this work and the subsequent flurry of anti-Pope satires moved him to provide a key which would presumably explain obscure references in the satire. In April, 1729, the second edition of the poem was offered to the public as the "Dunciad Variorum." The text of this version does not differ greatly from that of the first edition, but an elaborate apparatus of facetious annotation has been added. The satirical footnotes were written mostly by Pope, although it is possible that Richard Savage and William Cleland helped him. Some readers have considered the critical apparatus of the "Variorum" to be extraneous to the poem, but it is, in fact, an important part of it: the various appendages are a burlesque of the dull pedantry which Pope saw as a black cloud looming on the cultural and literary horizon.

The text of these two editions consists of three books. In Book I, the Goddess of Dullness (the first edition had been entitled in manuscript, "The Progress of Dulness") anoints Lewis Theobald as the King of the Dunces. Theobald, who had embarrassed Pope in 1726 by pointing out his deficiencies as a Shakespearean editor, is depicted as a pedantic critic, a Grub-street journalist, and a bad poet. The conception of this first book is quite close to that of Dryden's mock-heroic "MacFlecknoe," a poem which also relates the eternal battle between wit and dullness in literature.

Professor Maynard Mack has commented on the way the mock-heroic quality of the poem arises from the juxtaposition of metaphoric planes.[3] One of these is founded on echoes from the epics of the past, which serve as a structural image for the theme of the whole poem: the dissolution of literary and human values in the present (the eighteenth century). This plane is a serious one; but it is mocked by a second, more specific level, which is essentially comic in that it records the foolish and trivial activities of the dunces. The second, comic plane constantly degrades the first, serious one just as, for example, the diving games in Book II degrade the heroic ideals of the past. But, by tarnishing values held by the past, the second plane reinforces the serious purpose of the first plane in that it passes critical judgment on society.

Pope achieves this mock-heroic juxtaposition by incident, verbal echo, rhyme, or cadence. More often, he creates the discrepancy by distorting epic language through the insertion of a single commonplace word or line, as in the second of the following: "High on a gorgeous seat, that far out-shone/Henley's gilt tub, or Flecknoe's Irish throne" (II, 1–2). The mock-heroic thus allows Pope to present through the alternation of tones the heroic ideal for society and to indicate how far short of those ideals present society has fallen. Because of the juxtaposition of these planes, "The Dunciad," although a serious and profound comment on human values, is at the same time one of the great comic poems in our language. Book II continues the mock-heroic tenor of the first book by parodying the funeral games of the *Aeneid.* Although it is parody, Book II makes a serious comment by implying that these games, honoring the coronation of the Dunce King, sound the funeral knell of culture and civilization. Pope's seeming obsession with obscenity and scatology not only makes the individual critics, poets, and booksellers more revolting but also underscores the breakdown of moral and cultural values. Theobald's speech to the Goddess in Book I (ll. 143–212), describing the literary values distorted by the worshipers of Dullness, is dramatized in Book II by the realistic dunces as they dive in excrement and compete in slime. Book III again parodies the epic: *Aeneid, vi* and *Paradise Lost, XI–XII.* Theobald's visit to the Hell of Dullness parallels Aeneas' journey to the underworld of Hades; but the journey is also a vision, reminiscent of the closing books of *Paradise Lost,* of the future when Dullness shall have established dominion over the world.

Pope continued to make minor revisions in successive editions of "The Dunciad" until 1742 when he published Book IV as "The New Dunciad: As it was Found in the Year 1741." This new book fulfilled the prophecies uttered in Book III. By this date Pope had written his "Imitations of Horace" and had seen much of his prophecy come true as a result of Walpole's restrictive and immoral policies. Book IV, then, celebrates the triumph of stupidity and mediocrity in the land. The dramatic situation of the book is a royal audience at which titles and awards are handed out to all who have helped establish Dullness as the supreme power. Pope, like John the Baptist, is a voice crying in the wilderness. Professor Wimsatt describes this book as a "kaleidoscopic twilight, a dusky Inferno . . . unequalled in Pope's work for the density, intricacy, and wide heterogeneity of its materials . . . and the pressure of wit under which they are amalgamated." [4] Having revised the four books in an attempt to unify them, Pope in October, 1743, published the entire poem as the "Greater Dunciad." In this final version, Colley Cibber replaces Lewis Theobald as the King of Dunces.

Even as early as the publication of the 1728 edition, there were readers who criticized the seeming lack of action in the poem.

Professor Aubrey L. Williams has studied this criticism, and his conclusions answer the many objections raised by critics from 1728 to the present.[5] In general, he points out that the action fulfills two functions: it gives a narrative progression and thus an external structure to the poem, and it creates a complexity which allows a maximum interplay of literary, moral, social, and cultural values. Pope was well aware that a reader, accustomed to heroic action on the part of a protagonist, might find the "Dunciad" static. In one of the prefaces, "Martinus Scriblerus of the Poem," he carefully distinguishes between the action of the poem and that of the protagonist. The action of the "Dunciad" is

the Removal of the Imperial seat of Dulness from the City to the polite world; as that of the Aeneid is the Removal of the empire of *Troy* to *Latium*. But as *Homer*, singing only the *Wrath* of *Achilles*, yet includes in his poem the whole history of the *Trojan* war, in like manner our author hath drawn into this single action the whole history of Dulness and her children. To this end she is represented at the very opening of the poem, taking a view of her forces, which are distinguish'd into these three kinds, Party writers, dull poets, and wild criticks. . . .

The *Fable* being thus according to best example one and entire, as contain'd in the proposition; the *Machinary* is a continued chain of Allegories, setting forth the whole power, ministry, and empire of Dulness, extended thro' her subordinate instruments, in all her various operations.

This is branched into *Episodes*, each of which hath its Moral apart, tho' all conducive to the main end.[6]

It seems obvious that Pope was not greatly concerned with the action of the hero. The very fact that he could without too much revision substitute Cibber for Theobald indicates the relative lack of importance he attached to the protagonist. His main interest was in the allusive nature of the poem's action as defined in "Martinus Scriblerus of the Poem." Martinus hints that the reader might well consider how the poet has imitated the action:

As it beareth the name of Epic, it is thereby subjected to such severe indispensable rules as are laid on all Neotericks, a strict imitation of the antient. . . . How exact that Imitation hath been in this piece, appeareth not only by its general strucure, but by particular allusions infinite, many whereof have escaped both the commentator and poet

himself; yea divers by his exceeding diligence are so alter'd and inter-
woven with the rest, that several have already been, and more will be,
by the ignorant abused, as altogether and originally his own.[7]

The eighteenth century still regarded the court and the aristoc-
racy as the standard-bearers of culture and as the guardians of
civilization. Since the action of the "Dunciad" is "the Removal of
the Imperial seat of Dulness" from the mercenary, middle-class,
vulgar city of London to the polite world (the court, the nobility), Pope portrays the negation of culture with its concomitant
degeneration of all related values, and also points to the betrayal
of noble aspirations by a court which should uphold them. Using
this action as a loose narrative framework, Pope constructs episodes which fit into the general structure but do not necessarily
follow each other logically. The episodes are often parodies of
incidents in the *Aeneid* and *Paradise Lost* but they are always
illustrative of the theme. For example, as Aeneas was removed
from Troy to Latium by his goddess-mother, so Theobald-Cibber is
removed from the city to the court by the goddess Dullness. Thus
the action of the *Aeneid* is mocked by that of the "Dunciad"; but
this action is only the spare frame for the allusions which cluster
about the goddess and offer Pope's major theme.

The goddess is the apotheosis of negation. She is the "Mighty
Mother," from whose dark womb "momentary Monsters" emerge
to inhabit her "wild Creation":

> Here she beholds the Chaos dark and deep,
> Where nameless Somethings in their causes sleep
>
> . . . .
>
> See all her progeny, illustrious sight!
> Behold, and count them, as they rise to light.
> As Berecynthia, while her offspring vye
> In homage to the Mother of the sky,
> Surveys around her, in the blest abode,
> An hundred sons, and ev'ry son a God:
> Not with less glory mighty Dulness crown'd,
> Shall take thro' Grub-street her triumphant round;

> And her Parnassus glancing o'er at once,
> Behold an hundred sons, and each a Dunce.
>   (I, 55–56; III, 129–38)[8]

The animal imagery, everywhere prominent, emphasizes the monstrous nature of these dunces who worship Dullness. They deny their kinship with the spiritual, upper half of nature, preferring to relate themselves to the lower animal realm only. The spiritual qualities of man which produce civilization, intellectual and cultural advances, and moral values are thus made unrealizable.

To stress the negative qualities of Dullness, the goddess is described as being enveloped in clouds, fogs, or mists which magnify her terrifying presence but do not reveal her face. She is amorphous, a void. Imagery drawn from *Paradise Lost* (II, 894–96) reinforces both this feeling about the goddess and the metaphoric implications of her significance. The "Daughter of Chaos and eternal Night," she has from "eldest time" exercised her "ancient right" to "rule, in native Anarchy, the mind" (I, 9–16).

Because the goddess is a key metaphor in the poem, her qualities metaphorically transfer themselves to her progeny and explain the actions of the bad critics, poets, and booksellers. As Dullness is obscured by fog and cloud, so the obscure dunces prefer the covering of darkness or night. Their actions and descriptions are associated with images of darkness. Cibber prays to the goddess:

> O! ever gracious to perplex'd mankind,
> Still spread a healing mist before the mind;
> And lest we err by Wit's wild dancing light,
> Secure us kindly in our native night.   (I, 173–76)

Seated on his throne as King of the Dunces, Cibber suffuses his court with his "anti-light" of dullness:

> All eyes direct their rays
> On him, and crowds turn Coxcombs as they gaze.
> His peers shine round him with reflected grace,
> New edge their dulness, and new bronze their face.
> So from the Sun's broad beam, in shallow urns
> Heav'ns twinkling Sparks draw light, and point their horns.
>   (II, 7–12)

This preoccupation with the traditional imagery of light and darkness supports the theme of the whole poem: that chaos and darkness threaten to blot out all of man's significant activity: Nor *public* Flame, nor *private*, dares to shine;/Nor *human* Spark is left, nor Glimpse *divine!*" (IV, 651–52). Although Pope seems to concern himself primarily with Dullness extinguishing the light of wit and thus allowing the army of duncical poets, critics, and book-sellers to "MAKE ONE MIGHTY DUNCIAD OF THE LAND" (IV, 604), he did not separate literature from morals, culture, politics, or religion. For civilization to exist, light must expel darkness in each of these interrelated areas. Dullness, in devitalizing literature, must inevitably bring with it deterioration in these other areas as well.

It is fitting, then, that almost all movement in the poem is downward. In Book II the dunces dive in filth and excrement, an action which is symbolic on several levels: they seek darkness and cover; they associate themselves with the animal level of existence; they subject literary and moral values to filth and thus threaten to reduce culture and civilization to a low level of mediocrity that is worse than out-and-out barbarism.

Such an action as this is an evil thing; and, to make unmistakable his attitude, Pope fills the "Dunciad" with imagery alluding to the anti-religious nature of the rise of Dullness, which is another "Fall" of man. The starting point is the first five verses of the Gospel according to St. John: "In the beginning was the Word, and the Word was with God, and the Word was God. The same was in the beginning with God. All things were made by him; and without him was not anything made that hath been made. In him was life; and the life was the light of men. And the light shineth in the darkness; and the darkness apprehended it not." As God created through the Word (the Logos, the Son of God), so the Goddess of Dullness (the daughter of Chaos and old Night) creates through her son, Colley Cibber, the Anti-Christ or anti-wit ("against the Word"). But, by associating Miltonic allusion with the goddess, Pope conveys the idea that what she creates through Cibber and her hundred dunce-sons is actually Un-creation. Once this basic metaphor is established, connotations continue to swirl about it until the flood of chaos eventually inundates the world. Cibber sits on a throne, identified by allusion with that of Satan in hell, and presides over the fallen angels in Pandemonium. His duncical followers are described in terms of Milton's fallen angels: "Then thick as Locusts black'ning all the ground" (IV, 397). Edmund Curll, one of the bookseller dunces who plunges into a mock-heroic race, utters language reminiscent of Satan's at the time that great seraph began his journey through Chaos to find and destroy a newly created world:

> Fear held them mute. Alone, untaught to fear,
> Stood dauntless Curll; 'Behold that rival here!
> 'The race by vigour, not by vaunts is won;
> 'So take the hindmost, Hell.'—He said, and run.
>
> . . . .
>
> On feet and wings, and flies, and wades, and hops;
> So lab'ring on, with shoulders, hands, and head,
> Wide as a wind-mill all his figures spread.
> (II, 57–60, 64–66)

Cibber's vision of that new world to be created by Dullness calls to mind the vision of a ruined world shown to the fallen Adam in *Paradise Lost*, XI–XII.

Biblical and theological allusions continually reinforce this concept of evil and diabolism loose in the world. Innumerable allusions of that kind reverse Christian theology to a point where God becomes Dullness; Creator becomes Un-creator; Christ becomes Anti-Christ; nature becomes un-nature; the coming of the Messiah becomes that of an Anti-Messiah; Dullness establishes a church; the Eucharist becomes the black mass; and the dunces become the priests of this religion worshiped in these "new heavens and new earth." [9]

This anti-millennium is described in Book IV, which is the fulfillment of Cibber's vision of the future in Book III. It is a nightmare world in which every value becomes an anti-value. In such a valueless world, for example, the older Renaissance concept of the Grand Tour as part of the education of a young man becomes the training of a fool in the vices of the world (IV, 281–330). Or, in this world of madness, kings, queens, and duchesses—representing a nobility which believes the standards of the dunces to be correct—behave in a grotesque and fantastically unregal manner. This is the world which receives Dullness as deity:

> She comes! she comes! the sable Throne behold
> Of *Night* Primaeval, and of *Chaos* old!
> Before her, *Fancy's* gilded clouds decay,
> And all its varying Rain-bows die away.
> *Wit* shoots in vain its momentary fires,
> The meteor drops, and in a flash expires.
> As one by one, at dread Medea's strain,
> The sick'ning stars fade off th' ethereal plain;
> As Argus' eyes by Hermes' wand opprest,
> Clos'd one by one to everlasting rest;
> Thus at her felt approach, and secret might,
> *Art* after *Art* goes out, and all is Night.   (IV, 629–40)

Negation triumphs so completely that even Dullness "yawn'd—All Nature nods" (IV, 605), and

> Lo! thy dread Empire, CHAOS! is restor'd;
> Light dies before thy uncreating word:
> Thy hand, great Anarch! lets the curtain fall;
> And Universal Darkness buries All.   (IV, 653–56)

The "Dunciad" of 1743 was Pope's last creative effort. He was already weakened by disease and he felt possibly he had no more to say after such a heavy indictment of man and society. Urged by William Warburton, he tried to revise his total work into a definitive edition; but death overtook him when he had completed the revisions of the "Essay on Criticism," the "Essay on Man," the "Dunciad," and the four "Ethic Epistles." The final irony is that this "death-bed" edition was suppressed because of the very follies Pope had castigated in his last great poem.[10]

II *Pope's Reputation and Contribution*

Few poets have enjoyed as much praise and prestige as did Alexander Pope in his own lifetime. And it was only twelve years after the poet's death that Joseph Warton published *Genius and Writings of Pope* (1756), which marked the beginning of a critical tradition which has ebbed and flowed down to the present day. It was inevitable that Pope's reputation would be submerged in the inundation of Romanticism, which was to obscure the literary achievements of his century. Even a critic like Matthew

Arnold, although he was aware that the Romantics did not fully appreciate Pope's poetry, would still characterize it as a "classic of our prose" in *The Study of Poetry* (1880). This evaluation marked the lowest ebb of Pope's reputation.

As the Romantic floodwaters receded and landmarks could again be distinguished, the solid rock of Pope's work was shown to have remained unmoved; and scholars began to build once more upon it as a foundation. Pope's reputation, both as man and poet, was more firmly buttressed during the second and third decades of the twentieth century. Austin Warren's *Alexander Pope as Critic and Humanist* (1929) presented the poet as a man of his own century. The next year, Edith Sitwell's biography, *Alexander Pope*, destroyed several of the abusive legends and distortions of fact which had clustered about his name. George Sherburn's monumental *Early Career of Alexander Pope* (1934) completed Miss Sitwell's task and restored the poet to full view as a warm human being and the great poet that he truly was. Geoffrey Tillotson in *The Poetry of Pope* (1938) directed attention to the poetic qualities inherent in Pope's poetry and thus opened new vistas, since then explored by such scholars and critics as Maynard Mack, George Sherburn, Robert Rogers, Earl Wasserman, Aubrey Williams, the editors of the *Twickenham Edition* of Pope's poetry, and many others.

It is fitting that Pope and his work should be the subject of a large number of studies; his contribution to English poetry is very great, indeed, and he is the most outstanding satirist and poet of reason in English literature. While his Gargantuan stature as satirist and ratiocinative poet can be explained in part by the intellectual demands of his age, the fuller explanation must be sought in the poet's universal depiction of human frailty and grandeur. Pope saw man as a social creature, fallen from his first innocence to a morally and politically corrupt condition. Even worse, man accepted his lot. Pope challenged this complacency; he satirized the vices and follies which had reduced man to this state; and he proclaimed a message of regeneration. No one who loves mankind can fail to be moved by Pope's vision of the human race either as it is or as it ought to be.

His vision, like that of all great poets, is total and profound. Pope's philosophy is not wholly of the eighteenth century: he brought to his poetry a fervent belief in the ideals of Renaissance culture and made them the basis of his view of life. He was one of the last great poets to envision man, society, and nature as one harmonious whole—a view completely untenable in the modern world fragmented into the irrational, the unconscious, and the subjective. Pope believed that the values derived from past civilization and culture were still alive. He therefore filled his poetry with allusions from the poets of the past; in so doing, he felt he was bringing the past to bear upon the present, in the belief that thus a quickening culture would be transmitted to his own day and to posterity.

In order to present precisely and accurately his vision and his message of reform, Pope took from Dryden the heroic couplet and made it the perfect instrument of communication. He hammered the couplet upon the anvil of his genius until it reflected nature's balance, order, and harmony—Pope's basic philosophic view— and filled it with nuances subtle enough to convey his slightest feeling or shading of belief. He brought the couplet to such perfection, complexity, and richness of texture that no poet could further refine it.

As satirist, as ratiocinative poet, and as consummate artist, Pope has no peer in English poetry.

Notes and References

Chapter One

1. An exception to this statement is Geoffrey Tillotson, who objects to this interpretation (*Pope and Human Nature* [Oxford, 1958], pp. 247–51) on the quite valid argument that Pope's early work was mature and moral. The general division, however, seems valid to me, especially if one sees the poetry written before 1717 as "moral" in a general sense (as expressing a moral view of the world) and the later poems as "moral" in a specific way (as consciously addressed to moral problems in the world).

2. S. W. Singer (*ed.*), *Anecdotes, Observations, and Characters of Books and Men. Collected from the Conversation of Mr. Pope, and other Eminent Persons of his Time*. By the Rev. Joseph Spence (London, 1858), pp. 209–10.

3. George Sherburn (*ed.*), *The Correspondence of Alexander Pope* (Oxford, 1956), Vol. I, p. 7.

4. *Anecdotes*, p. 236.

5. This relation of structural devices to theme is discussed in full by E. Audra and Aubrey Williams, *The Twickenham Edition of Alexander Pope* (London, 1961), Vol. I, pp. 50–55.

6. The two "schools" of pastoral poetry are discussed at length in J. E. Congleton, *Theories of Pastoral Poetry in England, 1684–1798* (Gainesville, Florida, 1952) and in the *Twickenham Edition*, I, 15–20. My indebtedness to these sources is obvious.

7. The *Twickenham Edition* notes that Pope's poem is a document in the ancients-and-moderns controversy, and that Pope's "choice of figures for his temple of Fame owes more to Sir William Temple than to Chaucer" (II, 225).

8. Two quite perceptive readers of Pope are in agreement on this point. William K. Wimsatt comments, "Only in a limited sense is he a successful poet in the organ tones of the *Messiah*. Pope's orientation was secular" (*Alexander Pope: Selected Poetry and Prose* [New York, 1951], p. xxi). Reuben A. Brower notes that in *Messiah*, material splen-

dor dominates spiritual qualities and concludes that Pope "seems to have no profound or personal religious feelings to express" (*Alexander Pope: The Poetry of Allusion* [Oxford, 1959], p. 40).

9. George Sherburn, *The Best of Pope* (New York, 1940), p. 388.

10. William K. Wimsatt, Jr. *Alexander Pope: Selected Poetry and Prose*, p. xxxiv.

11. Reuben A. Brower, *Alexander Pope: The Poetry of Allusion*, pp. 48–62.

12. Maynard Mack, "On Reading Pope," *College English*, VII (1945–6), 266.

13. *Twickenham Edition*, I, 133–4.

14. Earl Wasserman, *The Subtler Language* (Baltimore, 1959), Ch. IV. I am indebted to Professor Wasserman's essay for the following discussion of the poem.

15. A succinct discussion of the Chain of Being can be found in E. M. W. Tillyard, *The Elizabethan World Picture* (London, 1943). The fullest treatment is A. O. Lovejoy, *The Great Chain of Being* (Cambridge, Mass., 1936).

16. "Windsor Forest" is considerably more indebted to Milton's "Lycidas" than anyone has so far pointed out. Both poems are youthful poets' attempts to explain the nature of poetry and the poetic process; both treat the theme of metamorphosis; both rely on water imagery and the use of Ovid's myth of Arethusa for their resolution; and the verbal echoes from "Lycidas" in "Windsor Forest" are many.

17. The essay form, since its first appearance in English from the pen of Francis Bacon (1597), had developed mainly in prose. Its poetic counterpart had not been in existence long enough in England to establish a set form or a tradition for it. In general, the poetic essay tended to follow Horace's *Ars Poetica*, which the seventeenth and eighteenth centuries considered as relatively formless, hence the name "essay," meaning "an attempt, or trial." Various predecessors of Pope's "Essay" would be Vida, "Concerning the Art of Poetry" (1527); Boileau, "Art Poetique" (1674) and the Dryden-Soames translation of this work, "The Art of Poetry" (1683); the Earl of Roscommon, "An Essay on Translated Verse" (1680); John Oldham, "The Art of Poetry" (1681); and John Sheffield, "Essay upon Poetry" (1682). Although it was not generally recognized by Pope's age that Horace's poem had three vaguely defined parts, *poésis* (poetry), *poéma* (the poem), and *poetà* (the poet), it is possible that Pope perceived this and patterned his three-part "Essay" on Horace's structure, substituting criticism for poetry, the critic for the poet, and a history of criticism for the poem.

18. For a thorough treatment of this difficult problem see E. N. Hooker, "Pope on Wit: the *Essay on Criticism*," *Eighteenth Century*

Notes and References

English Literature: Modern Essays in Criticism (ed. James L. Clifford [New York, 1959], pp. 42–61; George Sherburn, *The Best of Pope* (New York, 1939), pp. 393–96; and William Empson, "Wit in the *Essay on Criticism*," in *The Structure of Complex Words* (Norfolk, Conn., 1951), pp. 84–100.

19. George Sherburn, *The Best of Pope*, pp. 394–95.

20. *Twickenham Edition*, III, i, lxx–lxxi.

21. Edward Hooker, "Pope on Wit: the *Essay on Criticism*," p. 53.

22. Mr. Arthur Fenner, Jr.'s article, "The Unity of Pope's *Essay on Criticism*," *Philological Quarterly*, xxxix (1960), 435–46, argues in an interesting fashion that the moral basis of the "Essay" provides its internal means of unity.

23. Since the authorship or collaboration of these works cannot be established in some instances, they are somewhat on the periphery of Pope's canon. It therefore seems more proper to list them and their date of publication here rather than in the bibliography. (1) *Annus Mirabilis*, probably by Pope and Arbuthnot (1722); (2) *A Complete Key to the last New Farce, The What D'ye Call It*, probably by Pope and Gay (1715); (3) *Dunciad Variorum*, by Pope (1729); (4) *Epistle to the Most Learned Doctor W——d——d*, probably by Gay and Arbuthnot (1722); (5) *Heroi-Comical Epistle in Defence of Punning* (1732); (6) *Key to the Lock. Or, A Treatise proving beyond all Contradiction, the dangerous Tendency of a late Poem, entitled, The Rape of the Lock, To Government and Religion. By Esdras Barnivelt, Apoth.*, by Pope (1715); (7) *Memoirs of P. P.*, possibly by Pope and Gay (1727); (8) *Memoirs of Martinus Scriblerus*, presumably the joint work of the Club, but probably largely the work of or revised by Pope and Arbuthnot (1741); (9) *Origine of Sciences*, by Pope, Parnell, and Arbuthnot (1732); (10) *Peri Bathous: of the Art of Sinking in Poetry*, by Pope, possibly aided by Arbuthnot (1728); (11) *Stradling versus Stiles*, by Pope and perhaps Fortescue (1741). It should be noted that Pope's *Dunciad*, Swift's *Gulliver's Travels*, and Gay's *Beggar's Opera* had their inception in the Scriblerus group.

24. Pope's *Works* (1751), IV, 26n.

25. See *Correspondence* I, 143–203 *passim*.

26. For a full discussion of this technique, see Geoffrey Tillotson (ed.), *Twickenham Edition*, II, 106–23.

27. Although it lies outside the poem, Pope's letter to Arabella Fermor, published with the "Rape," further explains the relation of sylph to coquette:

The Rosicrucians are a People I must bring You acquainted with.

The best Account I know of them is in a French Book call'd Le Comte de Gabalis, which both in its Title and Size is so like a *Novel*, that many of the Fair Sex have read it for one by Mistake. According to these Gentlemen, the four Elements are inhabited by Spirits, which they call *Sylphs, Gnomes, Nymphs,* and *Salamanders.* The *Gnomes,* or Daemons of Earth, delight in Mischief; but the *Sylphs,* whose Habitation is in the Air, are the best-conditioned Creatures imaginable. For they say, any Mortals may enjoy the most intimate Familiarities with these gentle Spirits, upon a Condition very easie to all true *Adepts,* an inviolate Preservation of Chastity.

28. Cleanth Brooks has developed this "divinity motif" in his study of "The Rape of the Lock" in "The Case of Miss Arabella Fermor," *The Well Wrought Urn* (New York, 1947), pp. 74–95. It is carried to its ultimate conclusions in Rebecca Parkin, *The Poetic Workmanship of Alexander Pope* (University of Minnesota Press, 1955).

29. The points made here, although noted by several critics, are drawn from the convincing argument of Aubrey L. Williams in "The 'Fall' of China and *The Rape of the Lock*," *Philological Quarterly,* XLI (1962), 412–25.

30. *Ibid.,* p. 423.

31. Earl R. Wasserman, *The Subtler Language,* p. 123.

32. "Epistle to Dr. Arbuthnot," ll. 340–41.

Chapter Two

1. *Anecdotes, Observations, and Characters of Books and Men,* p. 231.

2. *Ibid.,* pp. 110–12.

3. *Ibid.,* pp. 164, 214.

4. *Ibid.,* p. 205.

5. Douglas Knight's book, *Pope and the Heroic Tradition: A Critical Study of His "Iliad"* (Yale University Press, 1951), develops at length Pope's view of the epic as a "living poetic tradition which for him presented a complex world and human society at its richest." Any reader of Mr. Knight's book will recognize my indebtedness to it at some points in the following discussion.

6. *Ibid.,* pp. 34–35.

7. *The Art of Poetry,* translated by Edward H. Blakeney (London, 1928), ll. 44–47.

8. *Correspondence,* II, 140.

9. *Ibid.,* p. 24.

10. *Ibid.,* p. 117.

11. George Sherburn, *The Early Career of Alexander Pope,* p. 234.

12. *Correspondence*, II, 118.

13. "Pope's Taste in Shakespeare," *The Shakespeare Association* (Oxford, 1936).

Chapter Three

1. Robert W. Rogers, *The Major Satires of Alexander Pope* (Urbana, Ill., 1955), pp. 30–31.

2. *Anecdotes*, p. 12.

3. *Ibid.*, p. 103.

4. *Correspondence*, III, 445.

5. "The Augustans," *English Masterpieces* (Prentice-Hall, 1950), V, p. 2. Many of the ideas expressed in this chapter find their origin in Maynard Mack's definitive remarks on the "Essay."

6. Bertrand A. Goldgar's article, "Pope's Theory of the Passions: The Background of Epistle II of the *Essay on Man*," *Philological Quarterly*, XLI (1962), 730–43, gives an excellent summation of the intellectual traditions behind Pope's psychological concept.

7. "The Augustans," p. 29.

8. Professor Mack's introduction to the *Twickenham Edition* of the poem (III:I, xxvi–xxxi) discusses Pope's use of current ideas and the futility of trying to isolate single sources which influenced Pope's thinking: Leibnitz, Shaftesbury, Bolingbroke, or King.

9. "The Design," prefixed to all editions of the poem after 1734.

10. G. Wilson Knight, *Laureate of Peace: On the Genius of Alexander Pope* (London, 1954), pp. 169–71 *passim*.

11. See above, p. 76.

12. As Pope was preparing to send copies of this edition to his friends he commented: "I am like Socrates, distributing my Morality [*i.e.*, the "Epistles to Several Persons"] among my friends, just as I am dying." (*Correspondence*, IV, 525.)

13. Benjamin Boyce in his study *The Character-Sketches in Pope's Poems* (Durham, N.C., 1962) notes that between 1700 and 1744 Pope wrote "at least sixty sketches ranging in length from four lines to seventy lines."

14. *Correspondence*, III, 316.

15. *Ibid.*, 419, 423.

16. Sir Richard Temple (1675–1749) was made Viscount Cobham at the accession of George I. Although a Whig, he became estranged from Walpole over the South Sea debacle and became a leader of the Whig opposition. He and Pope were friends from about 1725 on and often visited together at Twickenham and Stowe.

17. Philip, Duke of Wharton (1698–1731), was a sympathizer with the Jacobite group but was won over to the Whig cause when he was

created duke in 1718. He returned to the support of the Pretender in 1726 and eventually was outlawed (1729); he died two years later while still in exile.

18. Geoffrey Tillotson, citing lines 271–72, wisely concludes: "Mankind appears as androgynous, and the principle of 'the all in each' is reasserted. In the first, then, of his two Essays [*i.e.*, "To Cobham"] it is mankind that is concerned, though his instances of Nature primary and secondary are on the whole instances tricked out with male particulars. The title of his second, 'Of the Characters of Women,' announces the drop from primary to secondary Nature, but since the secondary that it discovers exists in both women and males, climbs back to primary. Perhaps a subject so subtle is best left confused, or complicated." (*Pope and Human Nature* [Oxford, 1958], p. 130).

19. "The Augustans," p. 30.

20. See Jean Hagstrum, *The Sister Arts; The Tradition of Literary Pictorialism and English Poetry from Dryden to Gray* (Chicago, 1958), and Robert J. Allen, "Pope and the Sister Arts," *Pope and His Contemporaries: Essays Presented to George Sherburn*. Edited by J. L. Clifford and Louis A. Landa (Oxford, 1949), pp. 78–88.

21. Allen Bathurst (1685–1775), a friend of Swift, Congreve, and Prior, became acquainted with Pope as early as 1718. He was a Tory member of Parliament, and he was created a baron in 1712 and an earl in 1772. His passion for landscape gardening possibly recommended him to Pope.

22. Earl Wasserman, *Pope's Epistle to Bathurst* (Baltimore, 1960), p. 11. Professor Wasserman's editing and critical reading of the epistle make one of the most detailed, scholarly pieces of work on Pope ever published. It and Maynard Mack's edition of "An Essay on Man" will surely remain for years to come archetypes of Pope scholarship. Since there is little to be said about "To Bathurst" which Professor Wasserman has not already stated, my indebtedness to his edition is great.

23. *Correspondence*, III, 345.

24. Earl Wasserman, *Pope's Epistle to Bathurst*, p. 37.

25. Richard Boyle (1695–1753) succeeded to his father's title and became Earl of Burlington in 1704. He had studied architecture in Italy, where he became an admirer of Andrea Palladio (1518–1580) whose Classical style Burlington furthered in England. In fact he spent much of his great fortune in erecting public buildings. Pope, when his family moved to Chiswick in 1716, made the acquaintance of Burlington; the two men were friends until Pope's death.

26. Reuben Brower, *Alexander Pope: The Poetry of Allusion*, p. 246.

27. *Correspondence*, "Pope to Swift, c. 19 June, 1730," III, 117.

Chapter Four

1. *Correspondence*, III, p. 350, "Pope to Jonathan Richardson, 18 February, 1733." Richardson had mistaken the "Essay on Man" for the "idle poem" (the first "Imitation"), which Pope proposed to publish with his name to protect the anonymity of the "Essay."

2. *Ibid.*, p. 253, "Pope to John Caryll, 8 March 1733." The reference is to the first "Imitation."

3. *Ibid.*, p. 358, "Pope to Caryll, 20 March 1733." Refers to the second "Imitation."

4. *Ibid.*, p. 37.

5. See Maynard Mack's excellent discussion of the "persona" in "The Muse of Satire," *Yale Review*, XLI (1951), 80–92.

6. *Correspondence*, III, 423.

7. Reuben Brower, *Alexander Pope: The Poetry of Allusion*, p. 294.

8. *Correspondence*, III, 416–17.

9. *Ibid.*, 428.

10. Benjamin Boyce, *The Character-Sketches in Pope's Poems* (Durham, N.C., Duke University Press, 1962), p. 75.

11. George Lyttleton (1709–1773), an opposition Whig member of Parliament for twenty years from Okehampton, was Secretary to the Prince of Wales and later a Privy Councillor and Chancellor of the Exchequer. An amateur poet, Lyttleton was a patron of writers, especially of James Thomson and Henry Fielding, who dedicated *Tom Jones* to him. A letter from Pope to Swift (October 12, 1738) highly praises Lyttleton and indicates a close intimacy between Pope and the politician.

12. Henry Hume, better known as Lord Polwarth (1708–1794) and an opposition Whig member of Parliament for Berwick, had great debating skill which Walpole feared. In 1740 Polwarth succeeded to his father's title as Earl of Marchmont, and his talents were lost to the opposition when he moved to the House of Lords. Pope named him as one of the executors of his estate.

13. Sir William Wyndham (1687–1740), a member of the House of Commons and a devoted adherent of Bolingbroke's views on government. Under the Tories in 1713–14 he was Chancellor of the Exchequer. His death in 1740, along with Polwarth's elevation to the peerage, destroyed the opposition's chance to unseat Walpole.

14. William Pulteney (1684–1764), a Whig supporter of Walpole until he turned against the leader in 1721 when he was not given a ministerial post. He was always suspected of seeking selfish ends by Bolingbroke and later by Pope, who in the beginning of their relationship liked Pulteney. In the 1740's he became the Earl of Bath, but not before he helped to bring down Walpole in 1742.

15. John Carteret (1690–1763), later Earl Granville, was Secretary of State in 1721, and Lord Lieutenant of Ireland from 1724 to 1730. When he returned from Ireland he broke with Walpole, whom he hoped to succeed, and joined the opposition party. From contemporary references there seems to be little doubt that Carteret was a rank opportunist.

16. *Correspondence*, IV, 50–51.

17. Pope's intimacy with the Prince of Wales and the fact that he shared the Prince's hostility toward King George II is made obvious by a gift which Pope gave to the future ruler. Pope was fond of dogs and gave the same name, "Bounce," to a succession of pets. When one of them had a litter, he gave the Prince a puppy with the following pointed couplet engraved on its silver collar: "I am his Highness' dog at Kew; Pray tell me, sir, whose dog are you?"

18. William Murray (1705–1793), a lawyer and member of Parliament from Boroughbridge. His speech against Spanish attacks on English merchant ships established his fame. He later became Solicitor-General, then Attorney-General, and finally Lord Chief Justice. He was raised to the peerage as the first Earl of Mansfield.

19. Henry St. John (1678–1751), Viscount Bolingbroke. He had been Secretary of State in the Tory government of 1710; but, suffering disgrace at the accession of George I, Bolingbroke fled to France in 1715, where he remained studying philosophy until pardoned in 1723, at which time he returned to England and settled at Dawley Farm near Twickenham. Pope fell under the spell of his charm and brilliant conversation, as did most other men in the opposition group. He praises Bolingbroke highly in at least six of the "Imitations of Horace."

20. *Correspondence*, IV, 178. The letter is dated May 17, 1739.

21. As reprinted from the Warburton 1751 edition by the *Twickenham Edition*, IV, 327.

Chapter Five

1. George Sherburn, *The Best of Pope*, p. 450.

2. See Harold Williams, *The Poems of Jonathan Swift* (Oxford, 1937), II, 406.

3. "Wit and Poetry and Pope," *Pope and His Contemporaries. Essays Presented to George Sherburn.* Edited by James L. Clifford and Louis A. Landa (Oxford, 1949), pp. 20–40.

4. William K. Wimsatt, Jr. *Alexander Pope: Selected Poetry and Prose*, p. xlix.

5. Aubrey L. Williams, *Pope's Dunciad: A Study of its Meaning* (Baton Rouge, La., 1955). Professor Williams' book is the major study

published on the "Dunciad," and I have relied heavily on it in this chapter.

6. *Twickenham Edition,* V, edited by James Sutherland, p. 51.

7. *Ibid.,* p. 52.

8. All quotations are taken from the 1743 edition of the "Dunciad."

9. This inversion of the Christian metaphor is discussed in detail by Aubrey Williams, *Pope's Dunciad: A Study of its Meaning,* pp. 131–58.

10. James Sutherland discusses the various conjectures surrounding this complicated matter in *Twickenham Edition,* III: ii, xv–xvii.

Selected Bibliography

A full Alexander Pope bibliography would require a volume in itself. The titles which follow are, of necessity, highly selective.

PRIMARY SOURCES

Most of Pope's major works are contained in the definitive *Twickenham Edition*, published by Methuen & Co., Ltd. in England and by Yale University Press in the United States. Its volumes are as follows:

I: *Pastoral Poetry and The Essay on Criticism.* Edited by E. Audra and A. Williams. New Haven: Yale University Press, 1961.

II: *The Rape of the Lock and Other Poems.* Edited by Geoffrey Tillotson. London: Methuen & Co., Ltd., 1940.

III,i: *An Essay on Man.* Edited by Maynard Mack. New Haven: Yale University Press, 1951.

III,ii: *Epistles to Several Persons (Moral Essays).* Edited by F. W. Bateson. New Haven: Yale University Press, 1951.

IV: *Imitations of Horace with An Epistle to Dr. Arbuthnot and The Epilogue to the Satires.* Edited by John Butt. New Haven: Yale University Press, 1953.

V: *The Dunciad.* Edited by James Sutherland. New Haven: Yale University Press, 1953.

VI: *Minor Poems.* Edited by Norman Ault and John Butt. New Haven: Yale University Press, 1954.

This edition can be supplemented by the following works:

POPE, ALEXANDER. *Three Hours after Marriage.* London: B. Lintot, 1717. A farce written in collaboration with John Gay and Dr. Arbuthnot.

———. *The Iliad of Homer.* 6 vols. London: B. Lintot, 1715–1720.

———. *Thomas Parnell: Poems on Several Occasions.* London: B. Lintot, 1722.

———. *The Works of John Sheffield, Earl of Mulgrave, Marquis of Normandy, and Duke of Buckingham.* 2 vols. London: J. Barber, 1723.

————. *Works of Shakespear.* 6 vols. London: Jacob Tonson, 1723–1725.

————. *The Odyssey of Homer.* 5 vols. London: B. Lintot, 1725.

————. *The Correspondence of Alexander Pope.* Edited by George Sherburn. 5 vols. Oxford: Clarendon Press, 1956.

————. *The Prose Works.* Edited by Norman Ault. Oxford: B. Blackwell, 1936. The volume admits without convincing documentation some dubious works attributed to Pope by Mr. Ault.

SPENCE, JOSEPH. *Anecdotes, Observations, and Characters of Men.* Edited by S. W. Singer. London: W. H. Carpenter, 1858.

SECONDARY SOURCES

1. Biographical

BUTT, JOHN. "Pope Seen through His Letters." *Eighteenth-Century English Literature: Modern Essays in Criticism.* Edited by James L. Clifford. New York: Oxford University Press, 1959. The "Letters" reveal Pope to have been a kind, humane man and a true friend to many of his age, both great and lowly.

SHERBURN, GEORGE. "Pope on the Threshold of His Career," *Harvard Library Bulletin,* XIII (1959), 29–46. Concerns Sir William Trumbull's direction of Pope's early reading.

————. *The Early Career of Alexander Pope.* Oxford: Clarendon Press, 1934. With meticulous scholarship, objectivity, and wit, this biography traces the poet's life to 1727. A sequel, dealing with the latter half of Pope's career, is still lacking.

2. General Criticism and the History of Ideas

ALLEN, ROBERT J. "Pope and the Sister Arts." *Pope and His Contemporaries: Essays Presented to George Sherburn.* Edited by James L. Clifford and Louis A. Landa. Oxford: Clarendon Press, 1949. Discusses Pope's technical knowledge of painting and the images drawn from painting in his poetry.

BOYCE, BENJAMIN. *The Character-Sketches in Pope's Poems.* Durham, North Carolina: Duke University Press, 1962. Traces Pope's use of the character sketch from the early to the late poems, and notes the poet's modifications of the form to suit his immediate objectives.

BROWER, REUBEN A. *Alexander Pope: The Poetry of Allusion.* Oxford: Clarendon Press, 1959. A most sensitive reading of Pope's work, showing how the poet echoes through allusion classical influences, mainly Horatian.

BUTT, JOHN. "The Inspiration of Pope's Poetry," *Essays on the Eighteenth Century Presented to David Nichol Smith in Honour of His*

Seventieth Birthday. Oxford: Clarendon Press, 1945. Notes the many-layered richness of Pope's verse and emphasizes that this must be seen if one is to understand and enjoy the poetry.

————. "Pope's Taste in Shakespeare." *The Shakespeare Association.* Oxford: University Press, 1936. This monograph studies Pope's taste by noting deleted and "starred" quotable passages in the edition of Shakespeare.

CLARK, DONALD B. "The Italian Fame of Alexander Pope," *Modern Language Quarterly,* XXII (1961), 357–66. Concerning translations of Pope's poems into Italian, from the eighteenth century to the twentieth.

CONGLETON, J. E. *Theories of Pastoral Poetry in England, 1684–1798.* Gainesville, Florida: University of Florida Press, 1952. A fine study of the theory of the pastoral genre.

EDWARDS, THOMAS R., JR. *This Dark Estate: A Reading of Pope.* Berkeley, California: University of California Press, 1963. Argues that the earlier poems express a state of Augustan balance, while the later satires express conflict. Mr. Edwards gives penetrating analyses of many of the poems.

KNIGHT, G. WILSON. *Laureate of Peace: On the Genius of Alexander Pope.* London: Routledge & Paul, 1954. Interesting intuitive, near-mystical attempt to show that Pope's poetry "radiates living meanings today."

MACK, MAYNARD. "On Reading Pope," *College English,* VII (February, 1946), 271–2. A lucid article on the way to read Pope's metaphor and allusion to greater advantage.

————. "The Augustans," *English Masterpieces.* Vol. V. Englewood Cliffs, New Jersey: Prentice-Hall, Inc., 1961. Most perceptive introductory essays on "An Essay on Criticism," "The Rape of the Lock," "An Essay on Man," "Epistle to a Lady," "Epistle to Dr. Arbuthnot," and the "Epilogue to the Satires."

PARKIN, REBECCA P. *The Poetic Workmanship of Alexander Pope.* Minneapolis: University of Minnesota, 1955. A study of Pope's moral views in terms of his poetic techniques. A useful but quite technical discussion on such matters as "paradox," "irony," "antithesis," and other critical terms.

ROOT, ROBERT K. *The Poetical Career of Alexander Pope.* Princeton: Princeton University Press, 1938. A pioneering work in the movement to evaluate Pope properly as a poet.

SHERBURN, GEORGE. "Pope at Work." *Essays on the Eighteenth Century Presented to D. Nichol Smith.* Oxford: Clarendon Press, 1945. Discusses the manner in which Pope perfected his lines.

————. "Pope and the 'Great Shew of Nature.'" *The Seventeenth Cen-*

tury: Studies in the History of English Thought and Literature from Bacon to Pope by Richard Foster Jones and Others Writing in His Honor. Stanford: Stanford University Press, 1951. A discussion of Pope's use of "epithets" in his work.

――――. (ed.) *The Best of Pope.* New York: Ronald Press, rev. ed., 1940. Very helpful introduction and notes that relate the poetry to the ideas of the time.

TILLOTSON, GEOFFREY. *On the Poetry of Pope.* Oxford: Clarendon Press, 1938. One of the first studies of Pope's work to help bring about a revival of interest in the poet. Mr. Tillotson stresses the importance of "ambiguity" and "levels of meaning" in reading Pope.

――――. *Pope and Human Nature.* Oxford: Clarendon Press, 1958. Emphasizes Pope's concept of man and his moral nature.

WARREN, AUSTIN. *Alexander Pope as Critic and Humanist.* Princeton: Princeton University Press, 1929. Concentrates on the poet's major works, his critical theories, and his reading. Warren is one of the first modern critics to take Pope's age at its own valuation; in doing so, he prepared for the re-evaluation of the poetry.

WASSERMAN, EARL R. "Nature Moralized: the Divine Analogy in the Eighteenth Century," *English Literary History,* XX (1953), 39–76. Discusses the breakdown of the validity of the old analogies.

WIMSATT, WILLIAM K., JR. *Alexander Pope: Selected Poetry and Prose.* New York: Rinehart & Co., 1951, vii–liv. An introductory essay which presents, in its limited space, much information and perceptive insights into Pope's poetry.

3. Criticism Dealing with Individual Works

ADEN, JOHN M. " 'First Follow Nature': Strategy and Stratification in *An Essay on Criticism,*" *Journal of English and Germanic Philology,* LV (1956), 604–17. Discusses how the rhetorical method of the essay stresses the primacy of nature.

ALPERS, PAUL J. "Pope's *To Bathurst* and the Mandevillian State," *English Literary History,* XXV (1958), 23–42. Concerned with Pope's opposition to Mandeville and his difficulty in concluding this "Epistle."

EMPSON, WILLIAM. "Wit in the Essay on Criticism." *The Structure of Complex Words.* Norfolk, Connecticut: New Directions, 1951.

FENNER, ARTHUR, JR. "The Unity of Pope's *Essay on Criticism,*" *Philological Quarterly,* XXXIX (1960), 435–46. Argues that the emphasis on "Pride" establishes a moral view which gives unity to the whole of the "Essay on Criticism."

HOOKER, EDWARD N. "Pope on Wit: the Essay on Criticism." *The Sev-*

enteenth Century: Studies in the History of English Thought and Literature from Bacon to Pope, by Richard Foster Jones and Others Writing in His Honor. Stanford: Stanford University Press, 1951. A study which relates the word "wit" to the eighteenth-century literary and intellectual milieu.

KNIGHT, DOUGLAS. *Pope and the Heroic Tradition: A Critical Study of His "Iliad."* New Haven: Yale University Press, 1951. A fine study of Pope's translation of the *Iliad*, relating it to the poet's own views on the problems of poetic translation.

MENGEL, ELIAS F., JR. "Patterns of Imagery in Pope's *Arbuthnot*," *Publications of the Modern Language Association*, LXIX (1954), 189–97. Discusses the manner in which Pope uses patterns of animal and filth imagery to create a total metaphoric value for the poem.

MOORE, JOHN R. "*Windsor Forest* and William III," *Modern Language Notes*, LXVI (1951), 451–54. Discusses Pope's use of historical data in the first "hunting scene" of "Windsor Forest" and suggests the Tory bias beneath the material used.

ROGERS, ROBERT. *The Major Satires of Alexander Pope.* Illinois Studies in Language and Literature: Vol. 40. Urbana, Illinois, 1955. A major study of Pope's satiric poems which argues convincingly for the view that the satires are of a piece in that all rest on basic ethical assumptions of the poet.

TILLOTSON, GEOFFREY. "Lady Mary Wortley Montague and Pope's *Elegy to the Memory of an Unfortunate Lady*." *Review of English Studies*, XII (1936), 401–12. Argues for Lady Mary Wortley Montague as the "unfortunate lady" of the "Elegy."

TUVESON, ERNEST. "*An Essay on Man* and 'The Way of Ideas,' " *English Literary History*, XXVI (1959), 368–86. A rather convincing argument that Locke's ideas influenced Pope.

WASSERMAN, EARL R. *The Subtler Language.* Baltimore: Johns Hopkins University Press, 1959. In Chapter IV an excellent analysis of "Windsor Forest," bringing a Renaissance commentary to bear on the text of the poem.

———. *Pope's "Epistle to Bathurst": A Critical Reading with an Edition of the Manuscripts.* Baltimore: Johns Hopkins University Press, 1960. A most exhaustive and learned treatment of the "Epistle." The emphasis is on the Renaissance background of the ideas in the poem and the rhetorical devices used by the poet to express his argument.

WILLIAMS, AUBREY L. *Pope's "Dunciad": A Study of Its Meaning.* Baton Rouge, Louisiana: Louisiana State University Press, 1955.

Selected Bibliography

The most thorough treatment available of the poem. It studies the "Dunciad" from every possible point of view.

WIMSATT, WILLIAM K., JR. "The Game of Ombre in *The Rape of the Lock*," *Review of English Studies*, n.s.I. (1950), 136–43.

4. Versification and Poetic Techniques

OLSON, ELDER. "Rhetoric and the Appreciation of Pope," *Modern Philology*, XXXVII (1939), 13–35. This early study argues that Pope's poetry must be read in the light of traditional rhetoric, especially the poet's use of the dramatic speaker in his poems.

MACK, MAYNARD. "Wit and Poetry and Pope: Some Observations on his Imagery." *Pope and his Contemporaries. Essays presented to George Sherburn.* Oxford: Clarendon Press, 1949. An excellent discussion of the manner in which Pope used allusion as an equivalent for metaphor.

———. "The Muse of Satire," *Yale Review*, XLI (1951–52), 80–92. Concerns the poses which Pope's "dramatis personae" usually assume in the satires.

WALLERSTEIN, RUTH. "Development of the Rhetoric and Metre of the Heroic Couplet," *Publications of the Modern Language Association*, L (1935). A most discerning article on how the principles of rhetoric helped to establish the formal metrical pattern of the heroic couplet.

WILLIAMSON, GEORGE. "The Rhetorical Pattern of neo-Classical Wit," *Modern Philology*, XXXIII (1935), 55–81. One of the pioneer studies in the development of the neo-Classical "heroic couplet" and its union with rhetorical figures (such as "antithesis") from the Renaissance books on rhetoric.

WIMSATT, WILLIAM K., JR. "One Relation of Rhyme to Reason: Alexander Pope," *Modern Language Quarterly*, V (1944), 323–38. Highly technical but enlightening essay on the subtlety with which Pope fuses sound and sense in his rhymes.

———. "Rhetoric and Poems: The Example of Pope," *English Institute Essays* (New York, 1949), 179–207. Illuminating discussion of Pope's modification of traditional rhetorical figures in his poems.

Index

Index

821.53
Po 81 Yc

DATE DUE

MAR 6 '72	FEB 28 '72		
DEC 11 '77	DEC 7 '77		
DE 02 '80	NOV 26 '84		
DE 07 '84	DEC 3 '84		
GAYLORD			PRINTED IN U.S A.